" The Object Lessons series achieves something very close
to magic: the books take ordinary—even banal—objects
and animate them with a rich history of invention,
political struggle, science, and popular mythology. Filled
with fascinating details and conveyed in sharp, accessible
prose, the books make the everyday world come to life.
Be warned: once you've read a few of these, you'll start
walking around your house, picking up random objects,
and musing aloud: 'I wonder what the story is behind
this thing?'"

Steven Johnson, author of *Where Good Ideas
Come From* and *How We Got to Now*

" Object Lessons describes themselves as 'short, beautiful
books,' and to that, I'll say, amen. . . . If you read enough
Object Lessons books, you'll fill your head with plenty of
trivia to amaze and annoy your friends and loved ones—
caution recommended on pontificating on the objects
surrounding you. More importantly, though . . . they
inspire us to take a second look at parts of the everyday
that we've taken for granted. These are not so much
lessons about the objects themselves, but opportunities
for self-reflection and storytelling. They remind us that
we are surrounded by a wondrous world, as long as we
care to look.'"

John Warner, *The Chicago Tribune*

OBJECT LESSONS

A book series about the hidden lives of ordinary things.

Series Editors:

Ian Bogost and Christopher Schaberg

Advisory Board:

Sara Ahmed, Jane Bennett, Jeffrey Jerome Cohen,
Johanna Drucker, Raiford Guins, Graham Harman,
renée hoogland, Pam Houston, Eileen Joy, Douglas
Kahn, Daniel Miller, Esther Milne, Timothy Morton,
Kathleen Stewart, Nigel Thrift, Rob Walker, Michele White.

In association with

LOYOLA UNIVERSITY NEW ORLEANS   Georgia Tech | Center for Media Studies

BOOKS IN THE SERIES

burger

CAROL J. ADAMS

BLOOMSBURY ACADEMIC
NEW YORK • LONDON • OXFORD • NEW DELHI • SYDNEY

BLOOMSBURY ACADEMIC
Bloomsbury Publishing Inc
1385 Broadway, New York, NY 10018, USA

BLOOMSBURY, BLOOMSBURY ACADEMIC and the Diana logo
are trademarks of Bloomsbury Publishing Plc

First published in the United States of America 2018

Cover design: Alice Marwick

A catalog record for this book is available from the Library of Congress.

ISBN: PB: 978-1-5013-2946-3
ePDF: 978-1-5013-2945-6
eBook: 978-1-5013-2947-0

Series: Object Lessons

Typeset by Deanta Global Publishing Services, Chennai, India
Printed and bound in the United States of America

To find out more about our authors and books visit www.bloomsbury.com
and sign up for our newsletters.

in memory of Forrest Girod Nearing

CONTENTS

1 CITIZEN BURGER

Campaigning for President in 1992, William Jefferson Clinton proved himself to be the citizen's candidate by his penchant for hamburgers. *Burgher:* citizen of the city. There he would be, according to the press, stopping in for hamburgers at local diners. Bill Clinton, not just the citizen's candidate, he was the *citizen* candidate; he liked the average Joe's kind of food (not the sloppy joe kind of average joes; though they use a burger bun, they are not burgers). "It's the economy, stupid" was the mantra of the Clinton campaign. The burger is the citizen's economic food choice, the everyman's lowest common denominator.

His opponent, President George H. W. Bush, on the other hand, scion of a prominent New England family, with a banker father who became a senator, had been cast as out of touch with the average citizen of the United States. "Poor George," future Texas governor Ann Richards famously said in 1988, "he was born with a silver foot in his mouth." Not Bill Clinton: from the media reports one got a sense had been born with a hamburger in his mouth. And not a hamburger like President Lyndon Johnson's favorite hamburger in the mid-1960s made from $35-per-pound ground-up aged sirloin. (Factoring in inflation that would be about $280 in 2017.)

During Clinton's campaign for the presidency in 1992 and his early years in office, the hamburger was riding high, with estimates that "86.6 percent of all Americans* order[ed] some type of hamburger sandwich at least once in 1994."[1]

But the times they were a-changing. In 1993, the Boca Burger appeared, a veggie burger made from soy protein and wheat gluten. The hamburger-eating presidential candidate began to change his choice of burgers in his early years in the White House, when he began scarfing down Boca Burgers— huge quantities of which were being ordered by First Lady Hillary Clinton. (In six weeks in 1994, 4,000 Boca Burgers were purchased by the White House.) Some anxiety from animal flesh producers greeted the news of the Boca Burger's popularity at 1600 Pennsylvania Avenue. A spokesperson for the American Meat Institute (AMI) stated, "Nothing will replace the American hamburger. The AMI is confident that President Clinton is still eating plenty of real hamburger too."[2]

---

*The use of the term "American" to refer to the United States, while common, is inaccurate. *American* encompasses North, Central, and South America and therefore has been a misnomer all these years when it refers to something specific to the United States. This becomes even more complicated when the hamburger is labeled *the* "All-American food" when it is clearly only referring to the history and current foodways of the United States. While the term appears in this book, I wish to note its problematic presumptions.

By the time First Lady Hillary Clinton became presidential candidate Clinton, Bill Clinton proved the AMI wrong. He followed a predominantly vegan diet.

The hamburger, as both idea and food item, is tightly coiled within the experience of being citizens of the United States. It is seen as a democratic, inclusive food. Elizabeth Rozin invokes the pattern and rhythm of Emma Lazarus's poem on the Statue of Liberty, "Give me your tired, your poor, Your huddled masses yearning to breathe free." Rozin sings the praises not of freedom but of "finely particulate meat, ground or shredded or minced or chopped." It is easy to prepare, she says, but equally important, "It offers the full nutritional and sensory experiences of meat to everyone—the young, the old, the toothless, and the tired."[3]

Citizen Burger Bar in North Carolina proclaims "A DELICIOUS BURGER IS YOUR RIGHT." Following the trope, they identify the burger and beer as "essential liberties." Ray Kroc in *The Founder* gives a pep talk to the McDonald brothers—whom he will soon be undercutting—by echoing nationalist themes. He exhorts them, "Franchise the damn thing," adding "from sea to shining sea." He declares, "Do it for your country. Do it for America." He promises soon the Golden Arches will become just as, if not more, important than the cross on the church and the flag on the courthouse; McDonald's must aspire to be "the place where Americans come together to break bread." Why, "McDonald's could be the new American church."

Crosses. Flags. Arches. John Lee Hancock's movie represents Kroc's view that the franchising of McDonald's is a story of civic accomplishment: the hamburger, the cheap food that everyone could eat. It fit the hand of a child; it could be held in the hand while driving; truly, you did not need teeth to eat many versions. ("There is nothing at McDonald's that makes it necessary to have teeth," novelist and social critic Vance Bourjaily opined in the 1970s.)[4]

The hamburger owes its existence to the United States, in part because the United States was the animal-flesh-eating democracy of the nineteenth century. Per capita consumption of animal flesh far outpaced the European places most immigrants hailed from. The development of the hamburger in the twentieth century consolidated the association between democratic rights and animal-flesh eating. Six years before a McDonald's opened in East Berlin, in 1982 the German Democratic Republic (GDR) created a McDonald's-like fast-food-burger place called the "Grilletta." Before the Berlin Wall crumbled, the Soviet-run GDR desired to demonstrate its "with-it-ness" with a burger joint—offering, of course, a better burger than any in the West. They wanted to out-West the West.

In the pages that follow, I am not going to review all the ideas about the history of the hamburger. I will not wonder whether the rampaging Tartars eating their ground horsemeat created the hamburger's precursor. I won't speculate on whether European immigrants whose point of demarcation was Hamburg salted their animal flesh to keep it fresh and arrived at the United States having innovated the "hamburger." Or was it the sailors from Hamburg? Did Delmonico's serve a Hamburg steak in 1834? Much ink is spilled on these issues and many others, drawing on legends, vague historical facts, fakelore masquerading as folklore, secondary but not primary sources, word of mouth, and assertions by various cities and counties of their role in the history of the hamburger. Here a Hamburg steak (or Salisbury steak) evolves into hamburger, there an immigrant or sailor brings the hamburger along with their baggage, and dotted throughout the United States, we can find the very birthplace of the hamburger itself.

Forget about the Tartars and Hamburg steak and Salisbury steak and sausage and meatloaf and meatball and the ancient Chinese text with a recipe for a hamburger-like food; the hamburger's origin story must plainly be from *here*, not over *there*, before we export it over there.

The "Americanness" of the hamburger—Bobby Flay's "perfect sandwich," no "the perfect meal"[5]—arises from the Western expansion of the United States in the nineteenth century. This is when economic, geographic, and industrial factors combined to favor cow flesh over pig flesh, and to deliver this cow flesh to growing markets. Eating its sizzling, fatty bulk between buns fulfills the iconic role of the US consumer. As countless historians have shown, consumption itself is an aspect of the narrative of twentieth-century United States.

Being the citizen's food, the hamburger is celebrated by the citizen—in the form of food critics and culinary historians—with a "gee-whiz" tone. They find in its story a story of progress itself. Hamburger-eating historians of the burger see inevitability in the statistics that show the global reach of the hamburger. They gobble down its status, forwarding their own favorites, and so offering one further salute to the triumphalist rhetoric of the hamburger through personal testimony. They join the stories told by those who prevailed: Ray Kroc (McDonald's) in his 1977 autobiography, Billy Ingram (White Castle) in a talk in 1964, Jim McLamore (Burger King) in a posthumously published autobiography. With red-blooded tropes, the arc is upward, a teleological logic to the prevailing of the hamburger. Telling the history chronologically becomes a form of obeisance to the success of mass production. For them, the hamburger's history is juicy, not problematic.

The narrative that grants inevitability to the success of the hamburger is confirmed by the hamburger consumers themselves in their purchases.

But let's pause and recognize that, as the *Diner's Dictionary* succinctly states, "the concept of a small cake of minced beef, grilled or fried, is an ancient one" and the designation "hamburger" is a new name for an old food.[6] Before there were hamburgers, there were individual-portion-sized cutlets. *The Oxford Companion to Food* identifies the chop—"slices of meat in the size of individual portions"—as a forerunner of hamburger.[7] Like beta versus VHS (predigital technology if you are wondering), there were different hamburgers, for instance White Castle's square versus the traditional circle. But these iterations involved the reshaping of animal flesh to a more universal and consistent size with interchangeable parts. It is as "American," and industrialized, as Henry Ford's assembly line production model.

With our palates influenced by nostalgia, we experiment with our burgers, but often within limit. There remains something that *cannot* be a burger, depending on who is deciding: hamburger from cows or not, from animal flesh or not, with condiments or not, bun or not.

Toward the end of a very long evening in which Harold and Kumar overcome a variety of obstacles in their pursuit of a White Castle hamburger, Kumar makes a speech about the meaning of immigration to the United States. In his telling, hamburgers form the heart of being a citizen of the United States.

So you think this is just about the burgers, huh? Let me tell you, it's about far more than that. Our parents came to this country, escaping persecution, poverty, and hunger. Hunger, Harold. They were very, very hungry. They wanted to live in a land that treated them as equals, a land filled with hamburger stands. And not just one type of hamburger, okay? Hundreds of types with different sizes, toppings, and condiments. That land was America. America, Harold! America! Now, this is about achieving what our parents set out for. This

FIGURE 1 *Harold and Kumar Go to White Castle.*

is about the pursuit of happiness. This night . . . is about the American dream.

Inspired, they take a leap that brings them to the White Castle, and we soon see them at a table filled with those famous sliders. The symbolism of the hamburger may seem fixed (equal to the entire United States), yet Kumar did not consume White Castle hamburgers in the movie scenes. The actor who plays Kumar, Kal Penn (Kalpen Suresh Modi), is a vegetarian and ate veggie burgers. Ten years before White Castle introduced a vegetarian slider to its customers, they custom-made veggie sliders for Penn to consume as Kumar.

If Harold and Kumar traversed the United States in the 1970s with Charles Kuralt, they would have passed by (or passed up) bridge burgers, Cable burgers, Dixie burgers, Yankee Doodle burgers, Capital burgers, Penta burgers (inside the Pentagon). Or they might have chosen (or rejected): "grabba burgers, kinga burgers, lotta burgers, castle burgers, country burgers, bronco burgers, Broadway burgers, broiled burgers, beefnut burgers, bell burgers, plush burgers, prime burgers, flame burgers . . . dude burgers, char burgers, tall boy burgers, golden burgers, 747 jet burgers, whiz burgers, nifty burgers, and thing burgers."[8]

You can butter your burger and serve it on cornbread, or with peanut butter and bacon. Thanks to the *Paris Review,* you can make Ernest Hemingway's hamburger recipe (with garlic, capers, scallions, seasonings, and egg as binder). You can get your burger with Fritos (in Texas of course), or a hard-boiled egg,

The names and varieties suggest that hamburgers are pluralistic like the United States itself. It's working-class food elevated, served in places called Castles and Royal and King. In movies, really bad guys eat hamburgers (*Pulp Fiction*) and really good guys eat hamburgers (*American Graffiti*). But it turns out the whiteness of the characters of *American Graffiti* mirrored the whiteness of the servers at the diner. The original Mel's Diner used in *American Graffiti*, set in 1962, did not let blacks work at the counter in the early 1960s. (Oh, Sixties California nostalgia, how you do disappoint.)

The year 1962 was notable for another burger: Claes Oldenburg's *Giant Hamburger*. It was not made from animal flesh, but from canvas filled with foam rubber and cardboard boxes. The sculpture was sewn together by master seamstress Patty Mucha—*Patty*, reminding us of a burger's definition: it is a patty, usually circular in shape.

Oldenburg believed art should relate to everyday life, its realities, its objects. Hard objects he made soft. Large objects he made small. And small objects, like the burger, he made large. On January 27, 1967, the Art Gallery of Ontario purchased the *Floor Burger* (nee *Giant Hamburger*) for $2,000. Art students protested the purchase of Oldenburg's

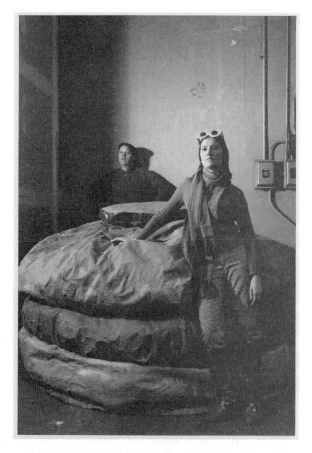

FIGURE 2 Claes Oldenburg and Patty Mucha at Oldenburg's studio-loft at 48 Howard Street.

Floor Burger, asking "What is art if this is art?" "What about a Heinz Ketchup bottle?" they challenged. They offered to donate a huge ketchup bottle to the art gallery—still hewing to the hamburger narrative, as ketchup is the preferred condiment. Maybe they should have asked, "What is a burger?"

Curators are found not only in art museums overseeing giant floor burgers; they can be found in restaurants where they are creating veggie burgers. "Sometimes you see veggie burgers made with 100 ingredients, a kitchen-sink burger," said Chloe Coscarelli, the chef and co-owner of Chloe's. "It's better when you curate a burger."[9]

The Oxford Companion of Food reminds us that "consumption of things like hamburger, that is, cooked round patties or rissoles of meat, dates back a very long way."[10] Burger, cutlet, rissole: they are not only made of animal flesh. Is the haggis waiting offstage to be transformed into the veggie burger? (Just kidding) Or is the falafel waiting simply a flattening into a patty? (More seriously.)

Like the fraught concept of citizen itself the burger is not one thing. Popeye subverted the idea of the hamburger in 1929 when spinach gave him (and anyone else who ate it) strength and the hamburger eater was the wimpy one. The Popeye cartoons were so popular during the Depression, sales of spinach in America increased by 33 percent. Now there are spinach burgers with or without hamburger.

The hamburger, long the "All-American" meal, has always contained an element of instability to it, not only because it can rot. From references in popular culture to investors like Bill Gates seeking to find the nonanimal burger that can feed the world, the burger's identity is as malleable as that patty of protein itself before it is thrown on a grill. Perhaps both the burger and the citizens it feeds are changing.

FIGURE 3 Richard Hess, "The Burger That's Eating New York," cover of *New York* magazine.

Credit: Painting by Richard Hess, HessDesignWorks.com

2 HAMBURGER

The history of the hamburger features a man, the Inventor, "American" of course. There he was toiling on his own, when he had a bright idea. The Edison of Fast Food, the Alexander Graham Bell of bread and animal flesh. The Edisons and the Bells consolidated their inventions through patents. Not so in the history of the hamburger. The Inventor is followed by the Innovator, who improves the product, who himself is followed by the capitalist, that is, the franchiser. The franchiser grasped the potential of the improvement, and goes into business with the innovator (or buys him out) becoming the capitalist par excellence by anticipating and shaping the consumers' desires. The franchiser would not be surprised that our language about wealth derives from cows. "The Roman scholar Varro Retains (116–27 BC) explained *Omnis pecuniae pecus fundamentum* ('for cattle are the origin of all money'—the Latin word for wealth, *pecunia,* comes from the word for cattle, *pecus*). The term 'cattle' is derived from the Middle English and Old Northern French *catel*, the late Latin *captale* and the Latin *capital,* meaning 'capital' in the sense of chattel or chief property."[1]

Contested "fathers"

The title of "first" has been asserted for inventors whose hamburger epiphanies occurred at a county fair or a lunch truck or a diner in Texas or New Haven. It is a national story, but also a local one. Take, for instance, "Hamburger Charlie"—Charles R. Nagreen—toiling at the Outagamie County Fair in Seymour, Wisconsin in October 1885. When people complained about greasy hands, Nagreen flattened meatballs between two pieces of bread. Seymour, Wisconsin, boasts that it is the "Home of the Hamburger." Or was it the Menches family, not in Wisconsin but western New York? In 1885, Frank, Charles, and Robert Menches, brothers and a nephew, took their food truck to the Buffalo Fair held in Hamburg. (You can see where this is leading.) Frank groundup sausage and they sold it as "a cooked meat patty" naming it *hamburg*er. Or did this happen at the Summit County Fair in Ohio?[2]

Like hamburgers, county fairs are iconic "American" institutions recalling and enacting "American" values. Toward the end of the nineteenth century, the county fair underwent "a period of radical readjustment."[3] For one, the number and kinds of amusements expanded (games of chance, horse racing rather than "speed trials," evening performances, carnivals). It was a time when agriculture became more mechanized, and fairs offered opportunities to see new machinery for farming. Fairs also became known as places with "interesting food that you can't get at home."[4]

The surprise is not that at least three county fairs compete for title of "birthplace" of the hamburger, but that more county fairs do not join in this pre-DNA paternity battle. Whether or not it really was invented at a county fair, it *had* to begin there. Before hamburgers became a symbol for the United States, the county fair was. What better way to prove how "American" the hamburger is than to place its birth in this historic "American" place? The fairgrounds guarantee the hamburger its "American" birthright. Ironically, the county fair, celebrator of all things agrarian, popularized a food related to industrialization.

Or the hamburger was born at a "lunch wagon." The lunch wagon could be set up outside of factories, and the hamburger's cheapness assured it became the workingman's friend. Claims are made for Louis' Lunch in New Haven as the inventor of the hamburger sandwich on white bread. In 1900, or so we are told, Louis Lassen was asked to serve a gentleman in a hurry so he put "ground steak trimmings between two slices of toast."[5] In 1974, Louis' Lunch was threatened with being bulldozed for development in New Haven, garnering *New York Times* coverage as "'Burger' birthplace"—though the quotation marks around "burger" suggested the *Times* questioned the claim.[6]

Still, such a claim from New Haven did not sit well with Texas businessman and Dallas Cowboys founder Clint Murchison, Jr., who supposedly said, "If we let the Yankees get away claiming the invention of hamburgers, they'll be going after chili next." Murchison argued that it was

Fletcher Davis from Athens, Texas, slinging hamburgers at a lunch counter set up on the courthouse square, who invented the hamburger.[7] Was it Davis who popularized this new food at the 1904 St. Louis World's Fair? Another supposed birthplace, the 1904 Fair popularized many foods: condensed milk, kumquats, ice cream cones, the hot dog, and the hamburger.

If not a fair or a lunch counter, the "American"-born hamburger is linked with other aspects of Americana. In 1891, Oscar Weber Bilby built a grill in Tulsa, Oklahoma, and prepared patties from cow flesh served between homemade sourdough buns made by his wife. Hundred people enjoyed this "first" hamburger.[8] The day? The fourth of July.

In the debate about whether the hamburger originated in western New York, Connecticut, Wisconsin, Ohio, Oklahoma, or Texas—claims often built on unsubstantiated assertions and/or proud family members' testimony—one point is clear: *Somewhere* in the United States the hamburger was born. The quarrel about where in the United States this happened serves to confirm its "American-ness." Though different claimants exist for creator of the hamburger, "American" ingenuity was the real father of the burger.

Innovators and capitalists

The hamburger's progress at the beginning of the twentieth century was not a continual arc of success. Upton Sinclair created the suspicion of animal flesh in his muckraking 1906 book, *The Jungle*:

> There were some jobs that it only paid to do once in a long time, and among these was the cleaning out of the waste barrels. Every spring they did it; and in the barrels would be dirt and rust and old nails and stale water—and cart load after cart load of it would be taken up and dumped in to the hoppers with fresh meat, and sent out to the public's breakfast.[9]

The book's descriptions of deplorable sanitation practices prompted the worry, "What does ground animal flesh *not* contain?"

Though Sinclair's work was an attempt to expose the situation of the worker, it prompted a crisis in consumption. Sinclair complained, "I aimed at the public's heart and by accident hit it in the stomach."[10] The result was the creation of the Food and Drug Administration and a suspicion of the contents of the hamburger. It would need rehabilitation.

White Castle

Professional cook Walter Anderson wanted a hamburger that was tasty. As his future partner reported, "When he wanted a sandwich for himself he would place a patty of meat on the griddle, flatten it with a spatula, mash some shredded onions into it, turn the patty over, place both halves of the bun over it to catch the heat, juices and aroma, and cook it for a short time on a hot fire."[11]

In 1916, Anderson bought an old shoe repair stand and began his own business, with his grill in sight of the restaurant customers. He then opened two more. Enter Billy Ingram who becomes his partner and together they opened the first US hamburger fast-food restaurant chain, White Castle, in 1921: *White* for purity, for cleanliness, and *Castle* for strength, to reassure the uneasy post-*Jungle* consumer.

The "White Castle System of Eating Houses Corporation" (founded 1924) introduced the standardization of food preparation, offering affordable food that could be carried out. As the hamburger itself mixed together fat and muscle, so the fast food "hamburger" began to make inroads toward homogenizing diverse ethnic foodways. White Castle's catchy slogan invited "Buy 'em by the sack," and people did. Billy Ingram was the Henry Ford of the hamburger, eventually buying Anderson out in 1933.

Privately owned White Castle tightly controlled expansion, allowing only company-owned stores. This limited its growth but controlled its quality. Its success in standardizing food preparation and popularizing the hamburger despite *The Jungle's* legacy birthed imitators: White Clocks, White Crests, White Cups, White Diamonds, White Domes, White Hut, White Manna, White Midgets, White Palaces, White Spots, White Taverns, White Tower. If not building on the evocation of purity and cleanliness through the repetition of *white,* its imitators choose the second aspect, stability, with names like Silver Castles, Blue Castles, Kings Castles, Royal Castles, Blue Towers, or Red Beacons.[12]

"You want a franchise with that?" The McDonald Brothers and Ray Kroc

The hamburger as a *product* emerged during the transition from a culture of character and production to one of consumption and personality.[13] The hamburger *franchise* flourished during a post–Second World War period of "a stifling homogenization of cultural products."[14] Its success was "closely associated with post-war suburban growth, the expansion of the national highway system and a dramatic rise in working women."[15] In addition, it benefited from reasonable prices. "From the 1950s on, while steak tended generally to exceed pork and ham in price, hamburger prices were surprisingly uniform and lower than any form of pork."[16]

Richard and Maurice McDonald opened the McDonald Brothers Burger Bar Drive-In in 1937. Twenty female carhops took orders, delivered the food (hot dogs but not hamburgers), and collected the money. In 1940, the brothers moved their drive-in to a new location. After the Second World War, their target audience became families. In 1948, the brothers closed their business for three months. Bye, bye carhops! And china and flatware! They quadrupled the size of their former grill, specially designing it. They developed new kitchen instruments (a hand-held stainless pump dispenser, a portable stainless steel lazy Susan) and the food was served in papers bags, wrappers, and cups. (No more lost cutlery.) They reduced their menu by one-quarter of their former offerings: Nine items would be sold, and central to the menu was the hamburger and a cheeseburger. They standardized the condiments to ketchup, mustard, onions, and two pickles. Just as Henry Ford contributed to the fragmentation of the individual's work and productivity through the assembly line (inspired as it was by the disassembly line of Chicago slaughterhouses), so the workers in McDonald's found themselves with repetitive tasks on a hamburger-making assembly line. Culinary historian Andrew Smith calls it a "militarized production system."[17] The result for the consumer was that their food could be prepared in advance of an order.

A self-service window required people to get out of their cars to place this order. It also allowed children to order their own food. The McDonald brothers began building on the success of their model by licensing it in the early 1950s, selling twenty-one franchises. At the same time, Richard McDonald added two arches to an architect-designed rectangular slanting-roof building so that it would be visible to people in cars. The McDonalds asked a sign maker—George Dexter from a neon sign company—to make the arches. In 1953, those famous bright yellow arches first appeared.

Ray Kroc, a milkshake machine salesman, curious about the restaurant that ordered so many machines from his company, came, looked, and conquered. He told his triumphal story in an autobiography. *The Founder* now tells his story for the movie-going public. The Cliff Notes version might read like this: in 1954 Ray Kroc gained the right to be the exclusive distributor of franchises for the McDonald brothers. On March 2, 1955 he formed McDonald's System, Inc. and opened his first McDonald's restaurant in Des Plaines, Illinois. Conflicts between Kroc and the McDonald brothers ensued. He wanted to change design; he needed their permission to do so. His vision for franchising and theirs could not be reconciled. He bought them out and acquired the trademark, McDonald's, thus depriving them of listing their name on their own restaurant. Kroc opened a competing McDonald's across from them, and eventually their restaurant closed. In a further evisceration of the McDonald brothers' role, The Des Plaines location is claimed to be McDonald's #1.

Kroc was not an inventor like the McDonald brothers. In fact, "every food product he [Kroc] thought of introducing—and the list is long—bombed in the marketplace."[18] Most of the innovations associated with McDonald's came from franchisees: the double-decker Big Mac influenced by Californian Bob Wein's 1937 "invention" of the "Big Boy," the fish fillet, the egg McMuffin, and Ronald McDonald. It was also franchisees that began to disregard McDonald's hiring ban on women at the end of the 1960s.

Ah, but first Ray Kroc and Harry Sonneborn in the 1950s began developing a unique franchising arrangement. They sold only single-store franchises, not exclusive territories.

(The latter was an easier way to make money.) With the McDonald's system, if a franchisee underperformed, they would not gain other franchises; only successful franchisees would be able to expand.

In 1956, a subsidiary company owned by McDonald's, "Franchise Realty Corporation," was created to handle the land deals for franchisees. At first, Franchise Reality Corporation rented the land and passed the costs of rent, property insurance, and taxes to the franchisees using an elaborate formula that insured a profit. (For instance, they charged a security deposit, half of which would be refunded in the fifteenth year, giving them capital to use interest free.) Then they started buying, not renting, the land. Sonneborn was famous for saying McDonald's was more in the real estate business than the restaurant business.

The Founder shows Ray Kroc in front of his first McDonald's restaurant in Des Plaines, Illinois, kneeling and picking up soil. When he and Harry Sonneborn created the Franchise Reality Corporation, they controlled the land upon which all future McDonald's would be built. The movie returns to this scene, but the second time Kroc bends down, picks up the soil, and scatters it across a map of the United States.

In 1974, *New York Times* reporter Mimi Sheraton opined in her cover article on McDonald's for *New York* magazine (see cover on p. 14), "McDonald's food is irredeemably horrible, with no saving graces whatever." She is just beginning. "It is ground, kneaded, and extruded by heavy machinery that compacts it so that the texture is somewhat like that of a baloney sausage, and it becomes rubbery when cooked."[19] James Beard referred to McDonald's as "a great machine that belches forth hamburgers."[20] He was also known to say, "a McDonald's hamburger patty is a piece of meat without character." While the characterless hamburger conquered the United States, it ventured into the international market, too: from Canada in 1967 to Vatican City in 2016, with France, Turkey, China, Qatar and close to 120 other countries boasting McDonald's.

From InstaBurger to Burger King

When InstaBurger King was founded in Jacksonville in 1953, Florida was awash with other burger chains with a loyal market. The founders, Keith J. Kramer and Matthew Burns, innovated hamburger preparation with an automatic broiler that relied on "a chain conveyor system to transport hamburgers through the broiler in metal baskets."[21]

Dave Edgerton was the first franchisee of InstaBurger King, and in 1954 he went into business with Miami restaurateur Jim McLamore. They opened several restaurants in the Miami area. Unlike the other "capitalists" who helped extend a franchise, they each graduated from Cornell University's School of Hotel Administration.

Any benefit the mechanical innovation of the broiler brought to hamburger production was burdened by its design flaws that resulted in frequent malfunctioning. Edgerton redesigned the broiler to make it more functional.[22]

With outside investment, Edgerton and McLamore grew a few more stores, but they lacked the customer appeal of the other Florida burger joints. McLamore learned of a hamburger drive-in stand in Gainesville serving a quarter pound hamburger. Inspired to do the same, McLamore coined the term "Whopper," providing both a product and a brand—Burger King, Home of the Whopper.[23] In 1957, they began franchising restaurants with their new menu, new name, and redesigned broiler machine. Two years later, Edgerton and McLamore purchased the company. They manufactured and sold broilers to their franchisees, as well as food items through a commissary. In 1967, Pillsbury purchased Burger King, something McLamore came to regret. Over the years Burger King passed through the hands of conglomerates and investment firms. As of 2017, Restaurant Brands International, a Canadian-based company, owned it.

McLamore acknowledged with a touch of envy that McDonald's innovation of controlling the real estate upon which franchisees operated offered that company more control and more profits.[24]

The mid-to late twentieth century is replete with the founding of many other hamburger-centered franchises— Wendy's, Carl's, Hardee's, and some that failed to succeed. A sorcerer's apprentice of food joints springing from one basic idea: cheap animal flesh on a bun. Various chains innovated; for instance, Jack in the Box was the first chain to offer drive-through window service, beginning a new trend. After two years of research, Wendy's "Project Gold Hamburger" resulted in an updating of their hamburger recipe—"Dave's Hot 'N Juicy" featured fresh pickles, two slices of cheese, red, not white, onions, toasted buns, and a thicker patty. In 2013, Dave's burger helped the company surpass Burger King in sales "to become the second-largest burger chain in the country."[25]

Besides Burger King's acquisition by Pillsbury in 1967, other hamburger chains became subsumed within larger corporate structures, including Burger Chef (with 800 restaurants) bought by General Foods in 1967, and Jack in the Box, acquired by Ralston Purina in 1968. At the same time, the country's biggest food industry was meatpacking and processing; these entities were also being bought up by conglomerates and banks. Morgan, for instance, in the 1970s was the controlling financial group for the parent company of Swift (Esmark), John Morrell (United Brands), and American Beef Packers (GE Credit Corp.).[26]

By the mid-1970s, 40 percent of all cow flesh consumed in the United States was ground beef. The statistic for cow flesh consumed away from home was even greater—75 percent of it was sold as hamburger in 1997.[27] In 2014, nine billion servings of burgers were ordered in the United States.[28]

Consumer Reports asked consumers in 2014 to rate the hamburgers they purchased from least to most delicious. Of twenty burgers, McDonald's ranked the lowest, below Hardees, White Castle, and Carl's Jr. Other low-scoring burgers were those of Jack in the Box and Burger King.[29]

Of what is a hamburger made?

Of what is the hamburger—whether #20 on *Consumer Reports'* list or #1—made?

The US Department of Agriculture defines the hamburger by what it can contain. It

> shall consist of chopped fresh and/or frozen beef with or without the addition of beef fat as such and/or seasoning, shall not contain more than 30 percent fat, and shall not contain added water, phosphates, binders, or extenders. Beef cheek meat (trimmed beef cheeks) may be used in the preparation of hamburger only in accordance with the conditions prescribed in paragraph (a) of this section [that is, unlabeled if it is less than 25 percent of the total amount of the meat].[30]

If one is making a basic burger at home, recipes recommend *ground chuck + salt = basic burger.* Ground chuck is considered the cut of animal flesh that contains enough fat to add flavor and juiciness. Generally, this proportion is 80 percent lean and 20 percent fat. In the late 1950s, McDonald's developed a hamburger formula that was "83 percent lean chuck (shoulder) from grass-fed cattle and 17 percent choice plates (lower rib cage) from grain-fed cattle."[31]

Billy Ingram wanted for White Castle a balance between flavor and fat, too, so "In each city, we selected a meat supply house with great care and then insisted on two things: that only U. S. Government inspected beef be used for our hamburgers, and that it be ground in certain proportions from specific cuts to give body and substance to the hamburger and other cuts to give it flavor and the right amount of fat."

In a 1925 article in the *Wichita Eagle,* Ingram assured the public that they could trust his animal flesh: "Our meat must be delivered from the butcher shop from two to four times daily. All the left-over meat is sent back. Meat is never more than four of five hours from the butcher shop when fried into hamburgers."[32] He was reassuring his consumers that the cow's shoulder being ground into hamburger came only from freshly killed cows.

FIGURE 4 Jill Jones, "Their Days Are Numbered," 40" x 60" charcoal and pastel on mat board.

3 COW BURGER

Domesticated cows descend from the mighty aurochs, who stood six and a half feet at the shoulder—the part of the cow that would, millennia later, be targeted for the hamburger-eating public. About ten thousand years ago, aurochs evolved into three different domesticated strains: those found in Asia, those found in the Near East and Europe, and those found in Africa. European cave paintings from 17,000 BCE depict the aurochs. They became extinct in the fifteenth century due to hunting and the clearing of woodland for pasture for their domesticated cousins. At the end of the century, those cousins arrived in North America.

The cow comes to North America

The "All-American" hamburger's main ingredient is from colonialism. When the Spanish colonized the "New World," they brought along the cow. Columbus's second trip to the West Indies included "an unknown number of domesticated long-horned Spanish cattle, which he aimed to introduce to the island of Hispaniola (now the Dominican Republic)."[1] Europeans brought cows and so also cow-derived diseases, tuberculosis, rinderpest (measles), and cowpox (smallpox). "Having never been exposed to cattle or their diseases, the indigenous peoples soon succumbed to the germs."[2]

Elisabeth Rozin's *The Primal Cheeseburger* celebrates the arrival of the cow: "Columbus's landing in the Bahamas in 1492 was a jumpstart for the development of the cheeseburger, for the Americas, both North and South, contained vast virgin prairies and plains, a rich and seemingly limitless source of pasturage for domesticated cattle."[3] Actually, Rozin is wrong: What was viewed as a virgin prairie and plains to colonizers was already occupied by Native Americans, bison, prairie grass, and flowers.

Spanish conquistadors imported Iberian Peninsula cows to the southwest of what became the United States in the early 1500s. These Criollo were accustomed to a hot, dry climate. At the end of that century, a herd of 5,000 Criollo cows arrived in northern Mexico and the area that became New Mexico.[4] They were the ancestors of Texan Longhorn cows.

Like the Spaniards, the English brought cows to their colonies, starting with the Jamestown colony in Virginia in 1611.

These cattle were not only exported to provide milk, labour and meat for the settlers, but also came as symbols of what the English considered civilized life: it was thought that they could help build the English Empire. In 1656 the House of Burgesses ruled that to give a cow to the Indians "will be a step to civilizing them and to making them Christians." To gain their cow, the Indians had to present eight wolves' heads to the country officials and, in return, the cow could be used to cultivate their land; thus turning the Indians into settled, working farmers, rather than disordered, idle and chaotic hunters.[5,*]

The colonists' relationship to the land differed from that of Native Americans. Environmental historian William Cronon explains:

> Indian villages had depended for much of their meat and clothing on wild foraging mammals such as deer and moose, animals whose populations were much less concentrated than their domesticated successors. Because there had been fewer of them in a given amount of territory, they had required less food and they had a smaller ecological effect on the land that fed them. The livestock of the colonists, on the other hand, required more land than all other agricultural activities put together.[6]

With the arrival of farmed animals, wolves were exterminated and fences appeared throughout the countryside. Still, cows

---

*One quarrels with the use of language here. Surely the author does not truly believe the terms *disordered*, *idle,* and *chaotic* for Native Americans, though she failed to use quotation marks; she does use quotes for "civilized" in the next sentence.

often grazed on and destroyed the planted fields of Native Americans, requiring them eventually to fence their land to protect their crops from destruction.

The land-gobbling, forest-devouring nature of the colonists' cows continued as the colonists became citizens of the new United States at the end of the eighteenth century; cows are land-intensive. (Animal agriculture now occupies one-third of the landmass of the earth.) The change in use of land in the United States led eventually to soil exhaustion. Cronon describes how "the removal of the forest [for more pasture land], the increase in destructive floods, the soil compaction and close-cropping wrought by grazing animals, plowing—all served to increase erosion."[7]

As long ago as the 1860s, George Marsh voiced an early warning about the environmental impact of cow ranching: at that time, three times the number of "domestic quadrupeds" existed as humans "of the Union." Marsh wrote, "I have spoken of the needs of agriculture as a principle cause of the destruction of the forest, and of domestic cattle as particularly injurious to the growth of young trees. But these animals affect the forest, indirectly, in a still more important way, because the extent of cleared ground required for agricultural use depends very much on the number and kinds of the cattle bred."

Marsh also described the inefficiency of meat production:

The ground required to produce the grass and grain consumed in rearing and fattening a grazing quadruped, would yield a far larger amount of nutriment, if devoted to the growing of breadstuffs, than is furnished by his flesh; and, upon the whole, whatever advantages may be reaped from the breeding of domestic cattle, it is plain that the cleared land devoted to their sustenance in the originally wood part of the United States, after deducting a quantity sufficient to produce an amount of aliment equal to their flesh, still greatly exceed that cultivated for vegetables, directly consumed by the people of the same regions.[8]

Looking backward, we often cast the "opening" of the West, and with it the land upon which to graze cows, as the catalyst of the US meat-centered diet. But the English had been beefeaters for centuries. "With the exception of the Netherlands, England had the highest ratio of domestic animals per man and per cultivated acre anywhere in Europe."[9] In fact, many in the nineteenth century believed that colonial powers like England succeeded over non-Western countries because the English ate meat and the colonized ate rice. One nineteenth-century nutritionist made the case this way:

The rice-eating Hindoo and Chinese and the potato-eating Irish peasant are kept in subjection by the well-fed English. Of the various causes that contributed to the defeat of Napoleon at Waterloo, one of the chief was that for the first time he was brought face to face with the nation of beef-eaters, who stood still until they were killed.[10]

English beef-lovers were the precursors to United States hamburger-lovers. In *Barbed Wire*, Reviel Netz points out that "inhabitants of the northern Atlantic shared a dietary heritage that prized the flesh of bovines."[11] The result was that "in America, it was not the West that shaped the eastern diet; it was the eastern diet that shaped the West. The same elsewhere: that so much of the globe was now given over to growing cows was an expression of how much the world was governed from Boston, New York, London, and Berlin. No rice eaters, there."[12]

The cow after the Civil War

During the nineteenth century, the pig remained the most frequently eaten animal. Because of the "methods of preservation up to the 1870s—curing, pickling, salting— processed pork was more flavorsome than beef and was often to be trusted, especially in warmer regions, where fresh meat was not."[13] Salted beef was also much less appetizing.

In the middle of the nineteenth century, as Texans left their recently admitted-to-the-Union state to fight for the Confederacy in the Civil War, the longhorns they left behind proliferated. After the war, a trail began by which cows transported themselves to market. These post–Civil War self-transporting cows also fed and accessed water themselves as they were herded north to their deaths.

Centralizing slaughter

Carl Sandburg might have called Chicago "hog butcher of the world," but it became known as "The Great Bovine City of the World," butchering 21,000 cows a day. The Union Stock Yard in Chicago opened for business on Christmas Day 1865. Nine railroad companies converged at the stockyards, four miles from the city center. By 1868, 2,300 pens occupied a hundred acres. The stockyards also became a meeting place for Chicago-farmed animal dealers and meatpackers. "They established intricate new connections among grain farmers, stock raisers, and butchers, thereby creating a new corporate network that gradually seized responsibility for moving and processing animal flesh in all parts of North America."[14] Scottish and English capitalists got into the mix, investing in meatpacking and railroads, as the train became the vehicle for transporting farmed animal shipments.

Until the 1870s, the structure of Western meat production was "still largely atomistic" rather than consolidated, but railroads "expedited the trend toward greater centralization."[15] Railroads overcame both spatial constraints (natural waterways and canals) as well as seasonal (frozen rivers).

At first, live cows were sent east on trains. With the invention of refrigeration, an alternative to tinned meat was available. Refrigeration both lengthened the time for keeping a dead cow's body edible and enabled the cow's body parts to be shipped. It was cheaper to send butchered meat rather than an entire body as body parts weighed less. (Forty to fifty percent of a dead animal is considered inedible.) In taste and price, "fresh" cow flesh competed with pig flesh.[16] And the cow could be disassembled in Chicago, creating a profitable secondary market in cows' by-products, and incentivizing the development of monopolies. By 1916, "five firms (Armour, Swift, Wilson, Morris, and Cudahy) dominated the meat-packing industry," slaughtering slightly more "than 82% of all federally inspected cattle killed."[17]

The destruction of the buffalo

The near extermination of the buffalo after the Civil War contributed to the rise of the hamburger. Between twenty or thirty million bison lived on the Great Plains at the beginning of the nineteenth century. In the late summer, when herds of fifty to two hundred congregated, several thousands moved together "eddying and wheeling under a cloud of dust."[18]

As the Union Pacific and Kansas Pacific railroads expanded, hunters could get to where the bison were, firing their guns at the herds from the train cars. Then, "disastrously, in 1870 Philadelphia tanners perfected techniques for turning bison hides into a supple and attractive leather. The next year, all hell broke loose."[19] Environmental historian William Cronon reports, "Within four years of the appearance of the railroads and a market in tannable hides, well over four million bison died on the southern plains alone." Richard Dodge poetically evoked their demise: "The buffalo melted away like snow before a summer's sun."[20]

Gone were the herds—and sustenance for the Great Plains Indians. The extermination of the buffalo was one of the forces that pushed Native Americans onto the reservation. Eliminating the buffalo "was widely considered necessary to end the resistance of the Plains Indians," and Indians on reservations "now depended on the federal government for food." Millions of pounds of cow flesh annually were purchased by the Indian Department "to feed the reservation Indians [and] a number of important cattlemen laid the foundations of their large enterprises by securing lucrative government contracts."[21]

Barbed wire

The prairies and plains needed one more technology of violence to consolidate the gains *against* Native Americans and the buffalo and *for* cows: a reasonably priced, easy-to-transport fencing material. For a few years, cows grazed for free along federal land in the Midwest. "Large ranchers sought to eliminate their competitor's access to grazing land by buying up the areas around springs and streams, gaining control of surrounding territory that depended on these sources of water and hay."[22] They grazed out the native prairie grass and open range disappeared. Farmers and ranchers both wished to protect their interests by controlling the land—but wood for fencing was scarce.

In 1873, Joseph F. Glidden, an Illinois farmer, patented barbed wire. Called the "Devil's Rope" by Texas ranchers, "Its goal was to prevent the motion of cows; its function relied on violence; its success depended on deployment on a vast scale."[23] Unlike other fencing, it used the body of the fenced-in being against itself; the act of pressing into barbed wire caused injury. Reviel Netz offers a history of barbed wire and shows how "the history of the prevention of motion is therefore a history of force upon bodies: a history of violence and pain."[24] According to Netz, barbed wire changed the capacity of colonization to conquer space. Previous forms of colonization took place either rapidly over a small area of land or more slowly over an entire landmass. Barbed wire solved the colonizing challenge of conquering both space and time simultaneously. Cronon adds to this analysis about space and time. "The whole point of corporate meat-packing had been to systematize the market in animal flesh—to liberate it from nature and geography. . . . Geography no longer mattered very much except as a problem in management: time had conspired with capital to annihilate space."[25]

Prairie became pasture and a feedlot system emerged of fattening steers with corn before slaughter. In 1884 a depression ruined many companies that traded in animals; one of the results was the compressing of the time for cows to mature. The shortening continued over the next hundred years—from 5 to 6, to 3 to 4 years before 1900—and by the Second World War cows only ranged for 1 to 2 years. When the US Department of Agriculture developed a grading system for meat, it rewarded corn-feeding over grazing. The grading system "designated as 'choice,' meat that had intramuscular fat (i.e., was 'marbled')." Corn-fed cows added this fat more rapidly than forage-fed cows.[26]

Changes in use of land, violently achieved, opened the possibility for a new food product: the hamburger. In the twentieth century and continuing into the twenty-first, appropriation of land continued, this time in Latin America. Thus, "American beef consumption continues to rest upon the availability of grassland—but, now, as part of a process of international capitalist underdevelopment in which arable land is actually being converted to cattle pasture and being withdrawn from local subsistence production."[27] Destruction of the rain forest is a part of this conversion of land.

How to slaughter a cow

Some cows escape from slaughterhouses. Their desperate run through urban areas or hiding in a forest garners media attention and petitions for them to be spared. But most cows are dispatched within the slaughterhouse. The steps are relatively few. As a child, I watched cows being slaughtered. I grew up in a small village, and behind my father's law office was the local abattoir. "Butch" would shoot the cow in the head while inside a truck. The cow crumpled to the floor, a chain was attached to a back leg, and she was then pulled down a ramp with a pulley that lifted her up above the concrete floor. Her throat was cut, and blood drained out.

Upton Sinclair described the industrial slaughter at the beginning of the twentieth century:

> Along one side of the room ran a narrow gallery, a few feet from the floor, into which gallery the cattle were driven by men with goads which gave them electric shocks. Once crowded in here, the creatures were prisoned, each in a separate pen, by gates that shut, leaving them no room to turn around; and while they stood bellowing and plunging, over the top of the pen there leaned one of the "knockers," armed with a sledge hammer, and watching for a chance to deal a blow. The room echoed with the thuds in quick succession, and the stamping and kicking of the steers.[28]

One hundred years later, Eric Schlosser updated *The Jungle*: The "knocker" "welcomes cattle to the building. Cattle walk down a narrow chute and pause in front of him, blocked by a gate and then he shoots them in the head with a captive bolt stunner—a compressed-air gun attached to the ceiling by a long hose—which fire a steal bolt that knocks the cattle unconscious." A *pop, pop, pop* sound is heard. "As soon as the steer falls, a worker grabs one of its [sic] hind legs, shackles it [sic] to a chain, and the chain lifts the huge animal into the air."[29]

The "sticker" slits the neck of the steer. Every ten seconds, the sticker severs another steer's carotid artery. "He uses a long knife and must hit exactly the right spot to kill the animal humanely."

Then the cow is disassembled. "Knocker, Sticker, Shackler, Jumper, First Legger, Knuckle Dropper, Navel Boner, Splitter, Top/Bottom Butt, Feed Kill Chain—the names of job assignments at a modern slaughterhouse convey some of the brutality interned in the work."[30]

Peter Lovenheim described the slaughter of #13 at a small slaughterhouse that disassembled the cow by hand, not machine:

Suddenly, George slides open the door to the knocking pen. . . . There's a shuffling of hooves against the concrete floor. . . . George lifts the rifle, aims, and shoots. . . . Ed lifts the side of the knocking pen, and the steer rolls out the side. I can see the hole in his forehead. . . . He's a black Angus, with short horns that stick straight out to either side, and curly black hair on the top of his head, which flows forward to cover a tiny patch of white on his forehead. . . . Ed wraps a chain around 13's left hind hoof. With a screeching sound, a mechanical lift pulls the body up until 13's head hangs about a foot off the floor. His tongue hangs loosely from his mouth; clear fluid drips from his nose. Ed pushes 13 about eight feet along the overhead rail until he's positioned over a white barrel. Then, in a quick movement, George sticks 13 in the throat with a knife; as if a pipe had suddenly burst, a torrant of blood gushes from the wound. It has been less than two minutes since 13 entered the knocking pen. As his body hangs and bleeds, it shows no movement.[31]

A week later, Lovenheim made hamburgers from #13.

Since one-quarter of the nation's ground beef comes from "worn-out dairy cattle," as Schlosser calls them,[32] dairy farmers receive advice on "Helping You Maximize Dairy Market Cow Value." Due to genetic engineering, feed rations, and growth hormones, cows used in the dairy industry produce 61 percent more milk than cows from only twenty-five years ago. Their udders must carry an extra fifty-eight pounds of milk. The cow's bloated udders may force her hind legs apart, causing lameness. When dairy cows are sold at auction they may need to be prodded or poked to get them to walk. Some collapse and must be shot, thus removing them from the hamburger assembly line. The meat of culled dairy cows is leaner, allowing "McDonald's and other fast-food companies . . . [to] control the taste and texture of their ground beef by mixing relatively fatty meat from corn-fed animals" with the dead cow's meat.[33]

One dairy farmer told Peter Lovenheim, "'I like the way cows finish,' he says, 'They go right from productivity to death. One day they're productive animals and the next day they're hamburger.'"[34]

In 2002, Michael Pollan followed the life of one young black steer, #534. His goal was "to find out how a modern, industrial steak is produced in America these days, from insemination to slaughter."[35] When Pollan arrived at the slaughterhouse, he was blocked from entering. This meticulous researcher who, in *The Botany of Desire*, dutifully traveled to Europe to smoke pot and used a canoe to imitate Johnny Appleseed's entrance to Ohio, accepts the "do not enter" command. "The stunning, bleeding and evisceration process was off limits to a journalist, even a cattleman-journalist like myself."

Slaughter in the late twentieth century

In 1960, the Iowa Beef Packers opened its first slaughterhouse. Eric Schlosser describes the design:

> Applying the same labor principles to meatpacking that the McDonald brothers had applied to making hamburgers, Holman and Anderson designed a production system for their slaughterhouse in Denison, Iowa that eliminated the need for skilled workers. The new IBP plant was a one-story structure with a disassembly line. Each worker stood in one spot along the line, performing the same simple task over and over again, making the same knife cut thousands of times during an eight-hour shift.[36]

These new meatpacking industries, "with a fast-food mentality obsessed with throughout, efficiency, centralization, and control,"[37] benefited from new modes of transportation: the interstate highway system. They located in rural areas in Iowa, Kansas, Colorado, and Nebraska, nearer to feedlots and away from urban union strongholds.

During the Reagan years, independent meatpackers went out of business or were purchased by larger meatpackers. Antitrust laws to protect against monopolization and large meatpackers were deemed irrelevant as mergers concentrated the industry even more. ConAgra became the biggest meatpacker in 1987.

Those who work in these plants are a migrant industrial workforce. These workers are predominantly people of color living in low-income communities—about one-third from Latin America, where they were actively recruited by the corporations. When Schlosser reported on it, "two-thirds of the workers at the beef plant in Greeley cannot speak English." About half a million workers are employed in slaughterhouses in the United States with a turnover rate of about 100 percent a year. Some are undocumented workers whose status keeps them from reporting dangerous working environments or other violations of US laws.

"Line speed" refers to the speed at which animals are killed and processed. Workers are pressured to kill more and more animals in less and less time. Line speed is not regulated by federal worker safety laws, but by federal sanitation laws.[38]

Schlosser identified meatpacking as the most dangerous job in the United States. "The injury rate in a slaughterhouse is about three times higher than the rate in a typical

American factory."[39] Repetitive motion, long hours, lack of time to sharpen knives, pressure to increase speed combine to exacerbate the workers' risk of injury. "The workers suffer chronic pains in their hands, wrists, arms, shoulders and back" and many injuries go unreported. Workers may fear losing their job or being deported if they seek medical care. Complicating injury tracking is the fact "that the OSHA injury form was recently re-written to omit the category of repetitive stress injuries—the most commonly reported injury in the industry."

lauren Ornelas is the founder and executive director of Food Empowerment Project, a food justice not-for-profit that works with farmworkers and slaughterhouse workers. She pointed out, "In addition to low wages and a dangerous working environment, workers also face discrimination. There was a complaint filed at one slaughterhouse where workers who did not speak English were treated worse and not given the same breaks as English speakers. Interestingly enough, when these workers complained about their own rights being violated, they also reported mistreatment of the animals." She concluded, "Who grows up wanting to kill animals all day? No one."

Hamburger hill

The hamburger results from the triumph of technological modernism in factory farms and institutionalized slaughterhouses, and the vertical integration and globalization of animal agribusiness. It is the icon that can be eaten around the world with both a cow flesh delivery system and an attitude delivery system.

It was not until 1960 that cow flesh consumption in the United States outpaced pig flesh consumption: 85.1 pounds to 64.9 pounds. From 1960 on, cow flesh consumption increased, jumping from 85.1 pounds per capita in 1960 to 125.9 pounds per capita in 1977.[40]

During this time of transition from pig flesh to cow flesh, burger franchises multiplied and hamburger consumption became the "American Way." An interchangeability of bodies is central to hamburger production after the Second World War with the growth of "factory" feedlots. One hamburger can contain the DNA of more than a thousand cows.

A tragic illustration of the transition from dead pigs to dead cows and the interchangeability of bodies can be found in the way battles were nicknamed in the wars the United States fought after the Second World War. Infantry battles of the spring and summer of 1953 during the Korean War included the loss of more than 200 US soldiers' lives. Those battles were referred to as the Battle of Pork Chop Hill. Reflecting the rise of the hamburger from the early 1950s to 1968, Hamburger Hill is the name US soldiers in Vietnam gave to the mountain Dong Ap Bia during a days-long battle in May 1969.

The colonial figuration of the enemy as rice eaters makes its appearance, too, in descriptions of Hamburger Hill.

After the first assault on the mountain, fires dotting its side announced to the US soldiers that the North Vietnamese army "were cooking up a three- or four-day supply of rice, showing they were preparing for a long fight."[41]

With the North Vietnamese cooking their rice, US soldiers drew on their iconic food to describe their own experience. A short time after the four allied battalions secured Dong Ap Bia and were policing up the battlefield,

> a GI cut out the cardboard bottom of a C-ration box, printed the words "Hamburger Hill" on it, then nailed it to a charred, blasted tree trunk near the western edge of Hill 937. Another GI, passing by a short time later, added the words "Was it worth it?"[42]

Immediately after the battle, *Time* magazine said the name was "a grisly but all too appropriate description."[43] The generation of young men that would have hung out at burger joints and drive-ins chose this metaphor. The 1973 movie *American Graffiti*, completed near the end of the Vietnam War—with its depiction of hamburger diner culture of the early 1960s—recreated the lost world of young manhood at burger places. We learn at the end of the movie that Toad, one of the main male characters, was reported missing in action near An Lộc in December 1965. Its nostalgic evocation of the pre–Vietnam War time suggested not only that the burger joint was not what it once was, but that the young men who haunted it were no longer who they had been. The Vietnam

War intervened. Hamburger Hill captured both irretrievable, unrecoverable hamburgers and lives.

Twenty-first-century colonialism and patriarchal tropes

US literature often depicts the undeveloped land of the continental United States as female. *Virgin* land. When in 2008 Burger King introduced its ad campaign "Whopper Virgins," it drew on many of the tropes associated with the colonizing of the Great Plains. The premise of the advertisement was a taste-test comparison between Burger King's hamburger and McDonald's by people "who did not even have a word for hamburger." Ostensibly the search took the Burger King team into the far reaches of Thailand, Greenland, and "Transylvania."

In the first decade of the twenty-first century, Thailand was a popular sex tourism locale known for the availability of "fresh meat," that is, very young women and men. Burger King sweeps past this association, as it focuses on people in native dress, whose appearance in Greenland and Thailand represents the racial identity of those defeated by colonialism. Vasile Stănescu proposes that Transylvania (a region in Romania) was included to disingenuously prevent attacks on the ads for being racist. Burger King also produced a mock documentary about their taste test, which concludes with a food drop, implying that each of these peoples needed food aid (no hamburger = lack of food).

Whopper Virgins was just a new iteration of the old beliefs that associated the colonized with the feminized, and their non-beef-eating foodways required importing meat (as the United States army did to Native Americans on the Midwestern reservations). Stănescu suggests that the Whopper Virgins ad campaign "exoticized contemporary populations in order to recreate these xenophobic reasons for eating Western style meat and justify their imposition of fast food restaurants as their own type of pseudo-humanitarianism."[44]

The result? "This ad campaign was one of the most successful in Burger King's history, receiving multiple awards, significant web traffic, widespread media attention, and correlating with one of the largest stock price increases in the company's history." Stănescu argues that it was not the taste test, per se—the ostensible purpose of the ad—that created this success. The ad was successful because "the stereotypes between meat eating, gender, and xenophobia continue to resonate with a broad section of the public in the United States."[45]

Whopper Virgins used an old trope of the hamburger eater as masculinized colonizer who appropriates property, space, and life but added their own spin—eating a hamburger presented a new form of deflowering from the perspective of colonialism.

"Eat beef, the West wasn't won on a salad"—bumper sticker seen near Midwest slaughtering facilities

The indispensable aspect of the hamburger, its violence and its violent history, remains an unspoken ingredient in most discussions of the hamburger. The burger—minced, macerated, ground—is the renamed, reshaped food product furthest away from the animal. Violent processes probably inhere to all forms of food production, but with the hamburger it is imbricated throughout every ground-up striated muscle.

Why do the history and technologies of violence central to the hamburger remain unacknowledged? The violence could be invoked as a reminder of masculine identity and conservatism, something Pollan himself celebrates when he goes boar hunting. It could also have been claimed as part of the human identity.

True, the bovine is more pacific and in general less dangerous than a carnivore; killing a bovine might be seen as a less virile activity than killing carnivores. Still, a narrative of violence might have been developed to celebrate hamburger eating. The question becomes not how do we understand the violence at the heart of the hamburger, but why isn't the hamburger celebrated for the violence at its heart?

4 WOMAN BURGER

White Castle's Billy Ingram described the problem facing hamburger sellers in the early twentieth century: women did not trust pre-ground hamburger. Ingram recalled how his mother resolved her suspicion of hamburgers. "Some of us, however, may remember that, when Mother wanted hamburger, she would innocently buy a pound or two of a certain cut of beef and then, as the butcher started to wrap it up, say, 'Would you mind grinding it for me?' and stand and watch him do it."[1]

Philip Roth's 1969 novel *Portnoy's Complaint* updated the type:

Who in the history of the world has been least able to deal with a woman's tears? My father. I am second. He says to me, "You heard your mother. Don't eat French fries with Melvin Weiner after school." "Or ever," she pleads.

"Or ever," my father says.
"Or hamburgers out," she pleads.
"Or hamburgers out," he says.

"*Hamburgers*," she says bitterly, just as she might say Hitler, "where they can put anything in the world in that they want—and he eats them. Jack, make him promise, before he gives himself a terrible tsura, and it's too late."[2]

The hysterical mother at home fears the contaminated hamburger, while the calm mother at the butcher shop asks for a cut of animal flesh to be ground. What distinguishes and unites them is the grinder.

The grinder

The undisputed central technology for converting a cut of cow flesh to hamburger is the grinder. The June 1978 cover of *Hustler* magazine presented an unusual summary of this technology of burger making. The cover shows the bottom half of a naked woman's torso going into a meat grinder, from which extrudes ground hamburger—woman burger, presumably. Under the headline "Last All-Meat Issue," the cover appears to respond to the magazine's critics. A quote from *Hustler* founder Larry Flynt flanks the woman-meat: "We will no longer hang women up like pieces of meat." Instead, it would appear, the publication will start grinding them up like hamburger. *Hustler* accurately answers the question, "What is a hamburger?" A being transformed through technology from body parts to ground flesh, whether literal or figurative.

FIGURE 5 Kristin Rogers Brown, "Red," Bitch Media.
Cover by Kristin Rogers Brown.
Courtesy of Bitch Media.

The magazine amplified a metaphor from trench warfare: *the meat grinder* was the nickname soldiers in the First World War gave to the bloody Battle of Verdun. *Grinds me down* and *ground down* are metaphors for defeat. A human body going through a meat grinder is clearly defeated. *Hustler* speaks in stereotypes, not just about women, sexuality, and objectification, but about what a hamburger is: transformation of living into dead, of body parts into minced animal flesh—the ultimate victory of human over nonhuman animal.

The home grinder boasts a tray to hold the animal flesh, a corkscrew-looking auger, a blade, and plates—the discs covered in holes of various sizes which determine the size of the extruded ground animal flesh, graduated from coarse to fine. Grind hamburger with a coarse plate.

Hustler's cover misrepresents the process of grinding. First, the woman would have been cut into small pieces—usually the preferred one-to-two-inch-wide pieces of flesh before entering the grinder. Some chefs suggest grinding the animal flesh twice to ensure the fat and muscle fibers are well blended. Other hamburger specialists put animal flesh through the grinder three times. And *never* before the day upon which the animal flesh will be eaten—hamburger must be ground fresh.

Pre-grinder technology included rocks, mallets, and metal choppers. But the grinder does not just flatten and mince. It macerates and camouflages, and in so doing hamburger can hide tough animal flesh. Jim Williams, president of Golden State Foods Corp., a supplier of hamburger to drive-ins in California, described some of the possible contents of hamburger: blood to cover up high amounts of fat; nitrates to keep it pink even though it was turning; cow's stomachs or cheeks to extend it.[3]

Grinding unites while it separates. Iowa Beef Packers added "grinders" to its plants to process enormous quantities of hamburger. As a result, Eric Schlosser explains, "A single fast food hamburger now contains meat from dozens or even hundreds of different cattle."[4] The grinder grinds out associations, making one mash-up from disparate pieces all ground together. It is not a melting pot; it is a grinder. *The Grind*: When we work, and work, and work at monotonous drudgework. *The old grind*: an oppressive, everyday routine. *To grind one's tool*: (said of men) to copulate. *Grind*: to rotate the hips in a sensual or erotic manner.[5] *Staying on the grind*: "to work hard, always be hustling, or otherwise engaged in money-making or woman-procuring activities."[6] *Vice* offers advice for gay men using the Grindr app: use it for hookups without boring formalities.[7]

The Fall 2011 "Red" issue of *Bitch* magazine offered an answer to the *Hustler* cover: a variety of objects enter a grinder out of which emerges red yarn. But the technology itself remains unchanged. They are still ground up, ground down—ground through and through.

The woman's burger

For women of the early twentieth century, the anonymous work of the grinder was the problem. Its work hid bad, old, and tough animal flesh, all of which disappeared into the hamburger. How then to get women to trust the hamburger seller?

Billy Ingram's White Castle solved the challenge in 1932 by creating a Betty Crocker-like figure named "Julia Joyce" (her real name was Ella Louise Agniel). She went from community to community with bags of White Castle hamburgers, visiting women's clubs and community organizations, and teaching middle-class women how to plan weekly menus with White Castle as the main course. She would joke "the way to a man's heart is through his stomach" and read to the club women Billy Ingrams's "White Castle Code" to confirm the strong moral commitment at the heart of the product. Then she invited the women to the nearest White Castle to see its sanitary conditions and food preparation techniques. And the women came. She invited them to inspect the grill, and behind-the-scenes spaces at White Castle. When they left, they carried with them bags filled with White Caste sliders.[8]

Ingram recognized women's responsibilities in the nuclear family for food preparation. In 1989, Arlie Hochschild coined the term "The Second Shift" to emphasize that even working women continued to perform most household work and childcare. Women's responsibilities at home concerned earlier feminists, too. In 1910, one husband challenged the local women's group, when he complained about his wife: "She is always cooking, or has just cooked, or is just going to cook, or is too tired from cooking. If there is a way out of this, with something to eat still in sight, for Heaven's sake, tell us!"[9]

Decades before the franchise system delivered hamburgers to the homes of wives and mothers, feminists identified "ways out of this": designing homes without kitchens, advocating for community kitchens, creating cooked-food services, producers' cooperatives, generally trying to envision how to liberate women from their lives as cooks—or else to pay them for their labor. In 1890, the YWCA began to operate cafeterias. Factory kitchens prepared dinners. In her 1898 book *Women and Economics*, the feminist Charlotte Perkins Gilman argued that employed women needed day care and cooked-food service. Soon she proposed designs for apartments that included a communal kitchen. She wrote, "Home, sweet home, has never meant housework, sweet housework."[10]

She was not alone. In *Redesigning the American Dream: The Future of Housing, Work, and Family Life*, Dolores Hayden describes how "almost all American women involved in politics between 1870 and 1930 saw domestic work and family life as important theoretical and practical issues." Material feminists "argued that no adequate theory of political economy could develop without full consideration of domestic work."[11] And along came White Castle, exhorting "Give Mother a 'Night Off'" by taking home a bag of White Castle Hamburgers."[12]

Feminists of the late 1890s also designed, and then advocated for, community play spaces. The lack of good day care for all children and the prevalence of traditional sex roles led mothers to want a place to relax with their kids. Of all fast food companies, McDonald's responded to this need first. Actually, a McDonald's franchisee, George Gabriel in the late 1960s in Bensalem, Pennsylvania introduced the first children's playground. Soon Playlands "became the new centerpiece of McDonald's strategy for dominating the children's market."[13] The McDonaldland play area also "could establish a theme for a McDonald's unit, putting some character into what was otherwise a relatively bland restaurant."[14] It did not approximate Gilman's proposal of day care and cooked-food service, but at McDonald's women could socialize with other moms, while their kids ate and played.

Mouths wide open: Woman as burger/woman eats burger

Over the years, violent fantasies about women have been prevalent in burger-oriented media: women as hamburgers desiring consumption or women consuming huge burgers. Pornography started the trend. *Hustler* is only one example of fixating on the idea of visually consuming a woman. Inside the issue whose cover showed a woman going through a grinder, one encounters a photo of a naked woman spread-eagled on a hamburger bun and lathered with ketchup.

What was pornographic in the 1980s had entered the mainstream by the twenty-first century. In a 2006 Super

FIGURE 6 Photograph taken in Harlem, New York City, 1989. Artist unknown.

Photo: Micha Warren Photography.

Bowl ad, Burger King brought *Hustler's* woman-as-burger fantasy to life, albeit in a G-rated way. Burger King's advertisement featured individual women each dressed as one part of hamburger fixings—patty, tomatoes, lettuce, onion, etc. The Burger King issues an order: "Ladies, make that burger." They willingly obey the commands of the man-king singing, "Our sole purpose is fulfilling your wishes…" With exclamations of discomfort, they jump on top of each other simulating the order of ingredients in a burger, becoming an extraordinarily large burger awaiting consumption.

Independent burger places recreate the fantasy of the woman burger in their own ads. Consumable women burgers appear as images in a local restaurant or as an advertisement in a neighborhood newspaper. The hamburger flesh itself remains feminized—meat to be consumed—but the entire product "hamburger" becomes masculinized. At first hamburgers were *king* sized, or maybe *super-king* sized. As the hamburger business grew, so did the size of the hamburger. Soon their names seemed to be recalling the way men discuss their erections:

The Thick Burger.
The Whopper.
The Big Mac.
Big Boy.
Chubby Boy.
Beefy Boy.
Super Boy.[15]

Hardee's and Carl's (they are both owned by the same company, CKE Enterprises) introduced a 1,400-calorie Monster Thickburger (urban slang for a long-lasting erection). Because hamburgers contain cholesterol and saturated fat that can clog arteries and cut off blood to the penis, the Thickburger consumers may need to switch to a "VIAGRA burger (rise to the occasion!)"[16] Elsewhere, in a clownish book ostensibly authored by Ronald McDonald, the famous mascot describes how his name functions as the butt of hundreds of jokes, claiming he is asked: "Where did they get the name Big Mac—or are you just bragging?"[17]

Given the double entendre of big hamburgers standing in for erections, it is no surprise that some companies advertise their fare via women who can cram a hamburger, a Thick Burger, a Whopper, a Big Boy, etc., into their mouths. Carl's Jr. makes repeated use of this trope of a woman's mouth stuffed with burger in an eternal return of the obsession that takes the fantasy into newly salacious areas. One advertisement for Hardee's demonstrated the size of their Monster Thickburger by showing a woman stuffing her fist into her mouth. Called "Fist Girl," it was dubbed "BJ Girl" and "Deep Throat" Burger on the web. These are not just fantasies of sex but of control and humiliation of women.[18]

Some of the "virgins" in Burger King's Whopper Virgins ad (pp. 50–51) did not know how to eat a hamburger. Their lack of familiarity with swallowing burgers only makes sense within a media context in which hypersexualized women know *exactly* what to do with a hamburger. Burger King, Carl's, and Hardees show bikini-wearing women opening their mouths wide to take in the burger, happily, lustily. *These* women are not virgins. *They* know how to eat. What should the sexually inexperienced Whopper Virgins do? The women show them: the exotic juxtaposed with the erotic.

The fast food hamburger industry floods popular culture with depictions of the sexual objectification of women. It suggests an anxiety, but an anxiety about what? Is it about the production of hamburger from slaughtered cow to macerated flesh? Or about feminism? Perhaps the Burger King and Carl's Jr. ads depicting large-breasted women eating burgers enact the nostalgia associated with conservative politics? They represent a longing for a time when sex roles were more determined and determinative, when ogling women was okay and women wanting to be ogled was the norm. John Berger famously said, "Men look at women. Women watch themselves being looked at."[19] One Carl's Jr. ad taught men exactly how to look at women when it showed a buxom white woman eating a burger as she walks through a farmer's market. One man's hose spurts out water and then stops, implying male orgasm. Andrew Puzder, then chief executive of CKE Restaurants, defended the salacious advertisements in a most American way, by claiming they were very American: "I like our ads. I like beautiful women eating burgers in bikinis. I think it's very American."[20]

All fast-food restaurants have high incidences of sexual harassment, but new research suggests that women at CKE Restaurants "face far higher levels of workplace sexual harassment than the industry average." The Restaurant Opportunities Center (ROC) United announced that about 40 percent of women in the fast-food industry reported sexual harassment. But for women working at CKE Restaurants, 66 percent of them told of being sexually harassed.[21]

If fast food were a family, Carl's Jr., Hardees, and Burger King would be the younger brothers, squabbling and joking about women's bodies, competing over who can be the grossest, creating a workplace climate unfriendly to women. Burger King ostensibly changed its marketing emphasis in 2010 and CKE in early 2017, but like the indiscretions of real youth today, their earlier iterations of woman burgers live on forever online.

In the face of all this, McDonald's remained the responsible older brother in the hamburger franchise family, presenting burgers as wholesome food for everyone. It even attempted to appeal more to women directly, even if in a stereotypical way—via salads aimed toward women. For a while, products like the Asian Chicken Salad "turned their business around," according to the media critic Bob Garfield.[22] But in more recent years, McDonald's cut back on advertising salads because they represented only 2 to 3 percent of sales.

In a video leaked from the archives of *Access Hollywood* to the *Washington Post* on October 7, 2016, then-presidential candidate Donald Trump talks about his right to consume women. "Just kiss don't wait . . . When you're a star, they let you do it. You can do anything. . . . Grab them by the pussy. You can do anything." The morning after Trump was elected President of the United States, a physician jogged past a Washington, DC McDonald's. Some good ol' boys eating their McDonald's food outside called to her, "Who owns your pussy now?" Ironically, McDonald's was the main hamburger chain that had not advertised hamburgers by suggesting that men in fact do own women's pussies. Did the freedom to sexually harass in public signal a new morning in America when even the traditionally family-oriented McDonald's hamburgers would be, one way or another, caught within men's longing to devour women?

FIGURE 7a "The Rendered." Harris Ranch feed lot, Coalinga, California. Harris Ranch is the largest feedlot for cows on the West Coast, "processing" up to 250,000 cows annually. From seventy to one hundred thousand cows at a time spend a quarter of a year adding 400 pounds to their bodies before being slaughtered. From the series "The Rendered."

5 CREUTZFELDT-JAKOB BURGER AND OTHER MODERNIST HAMBURGER IDENTITY CRISES

In 1996, a man walked into a London McDonald's and asked for a Creutzfeldt-Jakob burger.[1] This followed a March 20 announcement that a disease in cows, bovine spongiform encephalopathy (BSE), commonly known as "Mad Cow Disease," was possibly linked to a fatal human equivalent, Creutzfeldt-Jakob disease (CJD). The disclosure that BSE might have "jumped species" from cows to human beings through the eating of infected animal flesh caused shockwaves in the economy and emotions of many people in Western countries, specifically Great Britain. The announcement was a startling about-face after years in which the British government assured the public that British cow flesh was safe to consume.

FIGURE 7b "The Rendered."

Creutzfeldt-Jakob disease generally strikes elderly people. The cases of CJD that stimulated the 1996 controversy were very different from the textbook cases. Not only did CJD attack young people, but also, upon being autopsied, their brain tissue looked different—more like that of Alzheimer's sufferers than the classic "Swiss cheese" appearance associated with traditional cases of CJD. Since the incubation period for CJD is anywhere from ten to forty years, many formerly happy beefeaters now worried that there was a time bomb ticking in their systems that they were powerless to stop.

We might say that 1996 was a cultural moment when the normally absent referent status of the cow within the hamburger became known and discussed. In *The Sexual Politics of Meat*, I politicized the literary concept of the absent referent and applied it to animals used for food. Living animals are the absent referents in hamburger consumption in three ways. They are literally absent because they are dead. They are absent referents because when we eat animals we change the way we talk about them, not as dead animals but hamburger. The third way animals disappear is metaphorical; they become metaphors for describing people's experiences. In this metaphorical sense, the meaning of the absent referent derives from its application or reference to something else.[2]

The Mad Cow crisis made animals in their living and dying present and caused sales to plummet. To understand how humans might get CJD from eating cows, people learned about how cows had gotten BSE. Information on what herbivorous cows had been fed—the brains of other cows—and the sight of entire herds of cows being burned to stop the spread, shocked consumers.

The Mad Cow crisis was thought to be a body blow to the industry. McDonald's quickly added a veggie burger to their offerings in England. After the publication of *The Jungle* in 1906, people for a short time became, as humorist Finely Peter Dunne's "Mr. Dooley" described it, "viggytaryans."[3] But, in 1906, viggytaryans returned to eating animal flesh again, and after1996 the hamburger recovered from the scare.

How does cultural memory work with hamburgers? The Mad Cow crisis is but one of many identity crises the hamburger has undergone in its short, century-long career as a cheap, protein-based single food portion. Does a crisis provide opportunities to regain trust in the state though its reassurance that it will regulate animal flesh production, thus restoring both the product and populace to safety?

If there are Teflon Presidents—first said of Ronald Reagan because nothing stuck to him—let's consider that Teflon product, rebounding from identity crisis after identity crisis, to land back in the frying pan, Teflon-coated or not.

McLibel

The "McLibel Trial" provided a more serious body blow to the hamburger, and it was self-inflicted. The trial, the longest in English history (seven years), was prompted by McDonald's reaction to a six-page pamphlet distributed by London

FIGURE 8 Updated anti-McDonald's leaflet derived from the original London Greenpeace leaflet with original image.

Courtesy Roger Yates

Greenpeace (not an affiliate of the larger Greenpeace) in 1986 for "World Day of Action against McDonald's."

Of the many ironies associated with the trial, one stands out: only 2,000 original pamphlets were printed so it reached a limited populace. Writing in 1999, David Wolfson remarked, "Following the creation of the website 'McSpotlight,' a current version of the pamphlet was translated into a dozen languages, of which more than two million copies have been distributed worldwide."[4]

The pamphlet asked, "What's wrong with McDonald's?" It offered answers in several areas:

1 Exploiting its workers.

2 Manipulating children through advertising and marketing.

3 Destruction of the rainforest for the production of cattle.

4 Selling unhealthy food with a risk of cancer, heart disease, and food poisoning.

5 Cruelty toward animals.

6 Misrepresenting the amount of recycled papers used in food packaging.

By the time McDonald's brought a suit of defamation, both McDonald's and the British police infiltrated the group. At times, more infiltrators than activists probably attended the meetings.

The defamation law in England did not require McDonald's to prove that the information in the pamphlet was wrong nor that it was harmed by it. The burden was on the defendants to prove that what was said was correct, using primary sources (such as witnesses, first-hand accounts, and official documents). Legal aid is not available in England to defendants in cases of defamation. In the United States, First Amendment protections provide a "defense for individuals who criticize a 'public figure'" if they have restated information from reasonable sources such as "newspaper reports, books, films, or academic literature which they believe to be true." In England, the activists had no such protections.

Because of this pro-plaintiff law, McDonald's used the threat of such litigation in the past to elicit "apologies" from a variety of activists and news media. This time, McDonald's decided to sue five activists for their role in the pamphlet without approaching them first with a warning. Three out of five activists apologized, but two, Helen Steele, "a former London gardener and minibus driver, and Dave Morris, a single father and former postman" with a combined annual income of about $12,000, refused to comply.

When what you have to lose as an activist is your own sense of integrity, you are being asked to abandon what probably brought you into activism in the first place—a sense that something is wrong and change is needed. Steele and Moore would have to represent themselves and they did, in a trial that lasted seven years, with the help of some pro bono assistance along the way. Meanwhile, McDonalds spent over $16 million for attorneys. The results for McDonald's included bad public relations, no clear legal victory, and a sense that they incarnated the cartoon corporate plutocrat hiding behind a clown face depicted in the original flyer.

McDonald's did not let the defendants visit slaughterhouses or farms from which their animal flesh was sourced to prove claims of animal cruelty. Yet, the judge found that "the animals which became McDonald's products were cruelly treated and McDonald's was 'culpably responsible' for such treatment." Usually animal cruelty cases are confined to litigation within the current statutory definition about animal cruelty, and these laws often exempt standard farming practices from being defined as cruel. Until the McLibel case, animal activists faced a catch-22: How could they prove that farming practices were cruel to animals if the statutes excluded those very animals from protection, or so narrowly defined cruelty that it would not apply to the normal practices of contemporary farmers? By suing, McDonald's transformed the question of animal cruelty to "whether these practices were cruel in the view of a reasonable person." David Wolfson, a leading attorney in the field of animal law, summarizes the finding regarding animal cruelty:

> McDonald's argued a practice is cruel when it contravenes government or other official guidelines, recommendations, or codes; any practice which complies with these is not cruel. Mr. Justice Bell disagreed, recognizing a farming practice can be cruel, within the ordinary meaning of the word, even if it is legal. According to the court, while laws and government regulations are useful measures of animal welfare, neither is determinative of what is, or is not, a cruel practice. This is a significant determination. The fact that a court found so many common farming practices to be cruel, despite all of McDonald's advantages, leads to the conclusion that these practices will be considered cruel under any circumstance and should be prohibited.[5]

Two days after the verdict, 400,000 copies of an updated version of the pamphlet were distributed. McDonald's learned they could not un-ring the bell. They learned something else as well. Consumers continued to purchase their product. Bell? What bell?

Ag-Gag Laws

Passing of "Ag-Gag" laws that seek to impede and criminalize animal rights activism began in the early 1990s. Alicia Prygoski separates Ag-Gag laws into two parts: the early laws from the 1990s that were designed to deter animal rights activists from trespassing and causing physical property damage. These laws criminalized entering the premises of industrialized farming operations without permission and destroying or damaging property. They also contained language criminalizing any recording at industrialized farming operations.[6] The current laws, passed subsequent to 2011, "shifted away from preventing property damage to focusing primarily on banning recording in an effort to curb resulting economic damage."[7]

Besides Ag-Gag laws, there is the "Animal and Ecological Terrorism Act" (AETA). It was drafted by the conservative (and corporate-influenced[8]) American Legislative Exchange Council to expand "the definition of terrorism to include not only property destruction, but any action intended to 'deter' animal enterprises," including nonviolence, civil disobedience, witnessing and documenting corporate misconduct.[9]

Vegan congressman Dennis Kucinich spoke against the bill, pointing out that existing federal laws were adequate and that "trespassing is trespassing, theft is theft, harassment is harassment."[10] He forecast that "the bill created a special class of crimes for a specific type of protest, and such a broad terrorist label would chill free speech." In addition, "He also urged Congress to pay more attention to the issues raised by the millions of Americans concerned about the humane treatment of animals, and to consider legislation in response to those concerns."[11] Only a fraction of Congress was present to vote on AETA in the middle of the night, but it was passed, and signed into law by President George W. Bush on November 27, 2006. The result was that documenting animal abuse on factory farms by going undercover was illegal, but the animal abuse itself occupied a more fungible state. Some traditional acts of civil disobedience were now open to being labeled "terrorist."

The Oprah trial

In the 1990s in the United States, another legal strategy adopted to prevent criticism was food defamation laws, often called "veggie libel laws."

In 1996, after the announcement of the link between Mad Cow Disease and CJD, Oprah Winfrey hosted a show entitled "Dangerous Foods." Panelists included a National Cattlemen's Beef Association representative and Howard Lyman, a successful cow rancher transformed into a vegan advocate. Lyman said that the United States should ban the feeding of ruminants to ruminants and asserted that the United States was also at risk of an outbreak of Mad Cow Disease. As Lyman described animal flesh production, Oprah responded, "Cows are herbivores." She continued, "They shouldn't be eating other cows." Then she exclaimed, "It has just stopped me cold from eating another burger!" resulting in an "Oprah crash"—the price of cow flesh dropped to a ten-year low.

Texas cattlemen Paul F. Engler and Cactus Feeders, Inc. (Texas Beef Group) sued Winfrey and Lyman. On the first day of the trial, Texas vegans sent roses to Winfrey's hotel in Amarillo, welcoming her to the Lone Star state. The judge did not rule on the constitutionality of the law, but dismissed the case saying cows were not a perishable food and thus did not qualify for protection under the Texas law. (A year later the USDA banned the use of ruminant-to-ruminant feed supplements for cows.)

Lyman continues his advocacy of a vegan diet, remarking that those who sued them "apparently believe that the First Amendment . . . was not meant to be interpreted so broadly as to allow people to say unpleasant things about beef."[12]

Were any of these body blows to the hamburger? Not really; the hamburger shakes them off and rises again. Still, the 1990s illustrated a pattern of seeing information as so dangerous that it must be contained.

The day of the hooved locust

Cows, in Jeremy Rifkin's words, are "hooved locusts."[13] The newest threat to the hamburger is concern about the environmental consequences of raising and slaughtering these hooved locusts. News programs and articles appear on "What It Takes To Make A Quarter-Pound Hamburger" (examining demands on grain, water, land, and fossil fuel)[14] and "We are Killing the Environment One Hamburger at a Time" (ditto).[15] The question being posed by discussion of the environmental impact is "Where is the location of your citizenship? Are you a citizen of the earth?"

In 2006, the United Nations Food and Agriculture Organization produced its report "Livestock's Long Shadow." The report—considered conservative in its estimates by many environmental scholars—concluded that farmed animals produce more emissions than transportation ("18 percent of greenhouse gas emissions measured in CO_2 equivalent").[16]

I asked environmental philosopher Christopher Schlottmann, author with Jeff Sebo of *Food, Animals, and the Environment: An Ethical Approach* to guide me through the statistics about the environmental impacts of cows. He explained, "As with most life cycle analyses, there is no uncomplicated truth—any number is based on many assumptions or models."

He continued, "When we are talking about the environment, most often it is the impact animal agriculture has on land use change: clearing forests and digging up dirt causes erosion, nutrient loss, habitat destruction, and the release of carbon dioxide." This becomes the footprint of the agriculture product (like the hamburger): how much land was used, how much forest disappeared, the biodiversity that is lost as land is converted to pasture or crops for animals.

One thinks of one-third of the earth's land mass committed to animal agriculture.

There are about 1.5 billion cows and 60 billion land animals in all. "Visualize the weight of all the cows on earth," Schlottmann suggests. "It is greater than the weight of all the humans on earth, and each one of these cows is eating, respiring, defecating, trampling things." (A cow on a dairy farm produces about 150 pounds of waste every day.)

Schlottmann continued, "Cattle are responsible for a large part of greenhouse gases." The three main types of greenhouse

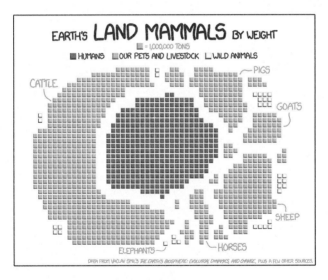

FIGURE 9 Land Mammals graphic.
Courtesy xkcd.com.

gas emissions are carbon dioxide, methane, and nitrous oxide emissions. "According to Ulf Sonesson of the Swedish Institute for Food and Biotechnology,"—I'm quoting Peter Singer here—"each kilogram of beef served is responsible for nineteen kilograms of carbon dioxide emissions, whereas each kilogram of potatoes served is responsible for only 280 grams—which makes beef sixty-seven times as carbon-intensive as potatoes."[17]

Methane is a product of the cow's digestion process; as a ruminant, the cow has a four-compartment stomach for digesting plants. One reporter interprets the digestive process in this way: "A cow takes plants, puts them into one acidic tank, processes it, puts it into another acidic tank and processes it, with tons of waste created along the way, not to mention greenhouse gases."[18] Both through burping and flatulence, the cow produces methane. Manure lagoons are also sources of methane. Most of us find it hard to aggregate a cow's bodily functions to their environmental consequences. But recall that number: 1.5 billion cows globally are burping and farting and defecating.

Some of the differences in statistics identifying the deleterious effects of raising cows versus other contributors to pollution like transportation arise from the length of the forecast: one hundred years or twenty years. From the perspective of the next century, Singer explains:

A ton of methane is generally regarded as twenty-five times more potent, in causing global warming, than a ton of carbon dioxide. That makes methane highly potent, but relative to carbon dioxide, this level of potency is heavily out-weighed by the very much smaller quantities of methane produced by ruminants, compared with the quantities of carbon dioxide produced by, say, coal-burning power stations. Hence methane emissions from ruminants are widely seen as being of much less concern than burning coal to generate electricity.

Schlottmann describes the problem with 100-year calculations: "With methane, two-thirds of it will be gone in ten years; and by the end of twenty years, 90 percent of it will have broken down." If we ask, "Which emissions will contribute to climate change in the next twenty years?" we can see how methane is far more heat trapping. Methane "holds 72 times more heat than carbon dioxide when calculated across twenty years."[19]

(And grass-fed cows who produce "organic" and "locavore" hamburgers release significantly more greenhouse gas.)

The third greenhouse gas that matters most is nitrous oxide, produced by fertilizer production and fertilizer use and by the mis-storage of animal waste. Farmers apply nitrogen fertilizer to crops to stimulate growth, but only half goes into the plants; the other half leaks into the environment. Animal agriculture is responsible for production and consumption of a large amount of plants and nitrogen-rich manure produced by cows. Schlottmann helped me understand the impact of this: "Fertilizer promotes plant life, but the fertilizer runoff in the water promotes algae growth, this sucks up all the oxygen in the water, leaving none for fish." Excess nitrogen causes algal bloom in water; it also threatens biodiversity, causes respiratory issues from air pollution, and health issues. According to one study, "raising beef produces almost 16 times as much nitrogen pollution as growing the same amount of bean protein."[20]

Concerns about water include both water pollution and water use. On an average a bovine uses 37 gallons of water a day. *Livestock's Long Shadow* reports,

> The livestock sector is a key player in increasing water use, accounting for over 8 percent of global human water use, mostly for the irrigation of feedcrops. It is probably the largest sectoral source of water pollution, contributing to eutrophication, "dead" zones in coastal areas, degradation of coral reefs, human health problems, emergence of antibiotic resistance and many others. The major sources of pollution are from animal wastes, antibiotics and hormones, chemicals from tanneries, fertilizers and pesticides used for feedcrops, and sediments from eroded pastures. Global figures are not available but in the United States, with the world's fourth largest land area, livestock are responsible for an estimated 55 percent of erosion and sediment, 37 percent of pesticide use, 50 percent of antibiotic use, and a third of the loads of nitrogen and phosphorus into freshwater resources.

Nick Fiddes observed that,

> Killing, cooking, and eating other animals' flesh provides perhaps the ultimate authentication of human superiority over the rest of nature, with the spilling of their blood a vibrant motif. Thus, for individuals and societies to whom environmental control is an important value, meat consumption is typically a key symbol. Meat has long stood for Man's proverbial "muscle" over the natural world.[21]

But it is not just muscle *over* the natural world; it is muscle *changing* the natural world.

Modernity and its discontents

During modernity the practice of taking food to feed to food prevailed, increasing animal flesh consumption by all classes in developed countries.[22] In most instances, feeding food to animals that become food reduces by 90 percent the available food for consumption. In other words, "less than ten percent of what cattle consume becomes part of their physical body."[23] Consider the soybean. Most of the soybean crop becomes food that we feed to food. Yet, the soybean, unlike cow flesh, makes little demand of land.

> Based on requirements of 70g protein per day, proteins from beef, [dairy] milk, wheat flour, and soybeans

cultivated by U.S. agricultural practices on one acre of land would meet such requirements for 77, 236, 526, and 2224 days, respectively. In other words, soybeans have the highest protein yield per acre, being about 4-fold more over wheat and about 29-fold more over beef.[24]

(A reminder of why one-third of the landmass of the earth is devoted to animal agriculture.)

Being disembodied, hamburgers lack the ability to remind us that cows breathe, eat, defecate, and as ruminants, burp. Eruptions of what is involved in the "burgerness" of the hamburger—the cow eating the brains of other cows (until 1996), the cow eating food that could go to humans, the cow defecating, burping, etc.—occur, but pass.

Eric Schlosser showed in *Fast Food Nation* how there was "shit in your meat" (fecal material brings with it pathogens like the deadly *E. coli 0156:H7*).[25] The federally subsidized animal industry produces animal flesh; people order hamburgers.

Morgan Spurlock eats himself sick on a month-long McDonald's diet in *Super Size Me*. The vertically integrated animal industry produces animal flesh; people order hamburgers.

Fears of antibiotic resistance and the presence of superbugs are raised, and with it the information that more than 50 percent of antibiotics are fed to domesticated animals.[26] The near-monopolistic animal industry produces animal flesh; people order hamburgers.

The modern success of the hamburger as it is located in consumers' practices and agribusiness's traditional income stream displaces whatever discontinuities various identity crises might prompt. Moreover, modernity favored grand narratives. And what a grand narrative it has had in the hamburger, especially when it ignores the federal subsidies and monopolies propping up the hamburger.

Is the hamburger an exhausted modernist relationship to space (land, air, and water), human-animal relationships, and food, with its hierarchy of control, its mastery of nonhuman animals and the earth? If the hamburger is the unsustainable modernist solution to protein delivery, what could take its place?

6 VEGGIE BURGER

Like the hamburger, the veggie burger has conflicting origin stories. A 2014 *Smithsonian* article traced the meatless burger only as far as 1982,[1] crediting a British inventor of a boxed veggie burger. Conservative US talk radio host Rush Limbaugh (who knew he was even interested?) credits the multinational food corporation Archer Daniels Midland in that same decade for creation of the veggie burger. These assertions prompted long-time vegetarians to scratch their heads; they remembered eating veggie burgers before that date.

Movie buffs might also have shown surprise at the placing of the veggie burger's origin to the 1980s. The 1955 Billy Wilder film *The Seven Year Itch* includes a scene in a vegetarian restaurant with a soyabean hamburger:

"Miss, may I have the check please?"

"Well now, let's see, you had the #7 Special: the Soyabean Hamburger with french-fried soybean, soybean sherbet, and peppermint tea."

"Don't forget I had a cocktail to start."

"Oh yes, you had the sauerkraut juice on the rocks. You'll be proud to know your entire meal with the cocktail was only 260 calories."

What would a soyabean burger of the mid-1950s have contained? Philip Chen's 1956 *Soybeans for Health, Longevity and Economy* offers one answer:

2 cups soybean pulp (ground or pressed through a sieve)
1 ¾ cups gluten [by which he meant a mixture commonly called "seitan"]
1 cup peanut butter
1 small onion
6 Tbs tomato sauce
2 Tbs soy sauce
½ tsp MSG
1 ½ t sage
4 t salt

(The 1982 "vegeburger" claimed as "first" by *Smithsonian* contained seitan and soy, too.)

But who would eat a soyabean burger in the 1950s?

Cranks

If an early definition of a veggie burger (and other vegetarian foods) might have been "something a vegetarian eats and no one else wants to" then, inevitably, the history of that burger is tied to the history of the vegetarian. The 1956 *Soybeans for Health, Longevity and Economy* suggested soyabean burgers were part of the answer to population growth, land scarcity, and health, but the Third Avenue vegetarian restaurant in *The Seven Year Itch* is portrayed as an environment for cranks, not social justice activists. Everyone eating at the vegetarian restaurant is shown to be dowdy or elderly, with bodies that definitely would not cause traffic to stop if one were standing above a grate in a white dress—the iconic image of Marilyn Monroe from *The Seven Year Itch*.

After enumerating the bill, the waitress launches into a speech, not about flesh eating, but nudity. She is for it. Clothes are the enemy; without clothes there would be no sickness, no war.

Vegetarian = "wacky" causes.

In her 1945 book on the soybean, in which she describes the soybean's potential role in food, flour, oil, clothing, medicine, and cosmetics, Mildred Lager observes, "For years, I have enjoyed the distinction of being classed as a 'bit queer,' a food crank, because I was interested in soybeans as a human food."[2]

A 1961 headline for the *Arizona Daily Star's* sports section announced, "Weights and wacky dieting." It described the menu of 6'7" javelin thrower Bob Shordone: eggs, raw carrot juice, organic fruit for lunch, and for dinner, "soya-burgers."[3]

Vegetarian = "wacky" causes, crank
therefore
Veggie and soy burgers = "wacky foods," unappetizing.

The *Smithsonian*'s misdating of the veggie burger is due to the hiddenness of the veggie burger's history. That hiddenness arises in part because the visible vegetarians of decades past were seen as isolated individuals holding odd (nondominant) cultural positions. That the veggie burger was considered to taste awful was connected to the stereotype of who ate it: the misfits. There's a reason one of the early 1960s popular natural health food restaurants in London called themselves "Cranks." The persistent presence of the veggie burger is lost within the stereotype of who would want to eat it. (And yes Cranks served soy burgers—"The whole food answer to the fast food craze!"[4])

The precursors of the veggie burger

People had been eating veggie burger-like creations for quite a while before the soyabean burger made its first appearance in a movie.

Just as the single-portion cutlet preceded the hamburger, the veggie cutlet preceded the meatless burger. *The Oxford Companion to Food* acknowledges this in one of its definitions of *cutlet:* "a round patty formed of minced meat (or a substitute, as in 'nut cutlet.')"[5] The English adopted the eighteenth-century French term, *croquette*—a compound of meat[6]—and vegetarians adapted the ball or rectangle-shaped croquette to their cuisine, coated it with breadcrumbs and fried it. The 1897 *Practical Vegetarian Cookery* offered a vegetable cutlet recipe and a Theosophical approach. Mrs. Roper's 1902 *Vegetable Cookery and Meat Substitutes* contained a recipe for bean croquettes.

M. R. L. Sharpe's 1908 *The Golden Rule Cookbook: Six Hundred Recipes for Meatless Dishes* provided directions for preparing lentil croquettes and nut croquettes, and included a recipe for a "Foundation Loaf."[7] Containing gluten (i.e., seitan), flavorings, and ground peanuts, it was steamed in a loaf mold, from which croquettes could be made.

Vegetarian George Bernard Shaw ate vegetable rissoles fried with breadcrumbs, nut croquettes, and nut cutlets made with Brazil nuts. Such non-meat combinations carried over to the veggie burger. For instance, Frances Moore Lappé offered a bean burger made of soybeans and peanuts in her 1971 *Diet for a Small Planet*.

Vegetarians did not have to mess with falafel, an extremely ancient, protein-loaded veggie croquette, or the centuries-old Indian fried vegetable patties (*tikkis*), deep-fried meat or vegetable balls (*kafta*), or protein-rich fried lentil or bean patties (*Badé*). As early as 2500 BCE, what might be seen as predecessors of the veggie burger were being prepared in South India: "early agriculture was based on indigenous millets and pulses, and involved large scale grinding, as well as ceramics for boiling. . . . It is perhaps no accident that in this region rice and other cereals are often ground to flour and mixed with pulse (*dhal*) flours to make many of the distinctive foods of this region, such as *idli* [a savory lentil-based single-portion cake], *vadai* [a lentil-based fritter or dumpling] *or dosa* [a lentil-based pancake]."[8] K. T. Achaya's *Indian Food: A Historical Companion* describes other early single-portion cakes made from mashed lentils and fried.[9]

According to soyfood experts William Shurtleff and Akiko Aoyagi, the first reference in English to the very popular Japanese *ganmodoki* ("mock-goose")—a deep-fried tofu burger—is found in 1924. Traditional preparation of *ganmodoki* involves pressing the tofu and mixing it with diced vegetables, sesame seeds, and other ingredients, shaping into patties, and then deep-frying.[10]

None of these precursors was a "veggie burger" per se, and yet each was a single-portion edible protein source that derived from plant-based sources and originated from non-"crank" populations.

The religious meatless burger

One US woman probably did more to catalyze the culinary development of the meatless burger than any other person. In the mid-nineteenth century, Ellen Gould White, founder of Seventh Day Adventism, had a vision that the Lord desired they "come out against intemperance of every kind"[11] and this intemperance included flesh eating. Her vision and subsequent writings created the first large-scale market for vegetarian products in the United States. To this day, about 50 percent of Seventh Day Adventists are vegetarian.

FIGURE 10 Madison Foods advertisement in the *Los Angeles Times*, March 7, 1941.

Courtesy Soyinfo Center, Lafayette, California.

By the 1890s, food inventors like John Harvey Kellogg and C. W. Post—and later institutions including Battle Creek, Loma Linda, Madison Foods, and Worthington Foods—focused on creating meatless alternatives. They were pioneers in developing meat analogs, cooking with seitan, and use of non-meat protein sources like nuts and soybeans.

As with the hamburger, the first sighting of a veggie burger-like product in the United States is in the late nineteenth century. In 1896 the Battle Creek Sanitarium Bakery introduced a canned product, "Nuttose," whose main ingredient was peanuts. It was "the first commercial meat alternative in the Western world."[12] It could be sliced into patties, fried, and served. Shortly after, Ella Eaton Kellogg provided a recipe for "Gluten patties" in her 1904 *Healthful Cookery: A collection of choice recipes for preparing foods, with special reference to health.*[13]

A largely invisible community with a largely invisible economy cultivated a meatless burger during the same decades that the hamburger emerged, and in the same places. Toward the end of the Depression, the Seventh Day Adventists launched a "Soy-Burger." It came from Madison Foods of Tennessee in 1937 and was renamed the Zoyburger two years later. In 1938, Loma Linda brought out a Gluten Burger (with Soy Flour).

Jethro Kloss's 1939 *Back to Eden: A Book On Herbal Remedies for Disease, and Other Natural Methods of Healing,* contained a recipe for both "Gluten Patties" and "Soy Patties" (combining soybean pulp, brown rice, onion, garlic, soy sauce, and vegetable fat). In 1941, Ida Klein, in a German book on vegetarian cookery, referred to a "meatless burger—'Patties made with soy flour.'"[14] And then the United States entered the war.

Second World War burger

On March 29, 1943, the Office of Price Administration established meat rationing. Meat rationing introduced "meatless days" when no animal flesh could be served by restaurants, rationing stamps for the purchase of meat, and many creative attempts to deal with animal flesh shortages. Not only were there "Meatless Tuesdays" but also soya flour was allowed to be added to hamburger meat.

White Castle explored serving meatless hamburger sandwiches.[15] Because of the more than forty years of food experimentation by Seventh Day Adventists, White Castle found several choices from which to select. White Castle's

Benny Benfer started exploring these alternatives even before rationing began and discovered a wide array of choices. He found that many major food producers were already marketing meatless sandwich patties, with John Harvey Kellogg's Battle Creek Foods offering the largest selection. Battle Creek offered two nonmeat patties, one made from yeast and vegetable juices and the other from wheat, peanuts, and salt. Columbus neighbor Special

Foods also offered a meat alternative named "Numete." It consisted of peanuts, corn flour, salt, and seasonings and was said to taste like beef.

The most abundant option was the soy burger offered by numerous companies. Loma Linda Foods offered "Vegelona"—a mixture of soybeans, tomatoes, onions, and peanuts—and "Proteena"—a concoction of soy, tomato juice, and yeast extract.[16]

During the Second World War, soybean production doubled. The *New York Times* described a "ten-cent soy burger" that could replace the hamburger on meatless days.[17] It also covered the appearance of "a mixture of soy grits, flour, dehydrated onions and other seasonings under the trade name Beanburger." The *Times* explained, "This powderlike preparation may be used 'as is' to make patties, or it may be employed as an extender for meat in hamburgers, croquettes, loaves, etc."[18] The *Los Angeles Times* followed two months later with their own coverage, referring to the bean burger as "meatless meat," the earliest English-language document so far known that uses that coinage.[19] At the same time, Butler's Vegeburger was introduced. The following year, as the war ended, Special Foods of Worthington, Ohio launched the Choplet-Burger, "a soy-based product sold in 30-ounce cans with a hamburger-like texture that could be shaped into patties and fried." Mildred Lager's 1945 *The Useful Soybean: A Plus Factor in Modern Living* included a recipe for "Vegetized ground soys" (ground soybeans, vegetable broth, tomato sauce, soy sauce, minced onion) from which you could make "soy burgers."

Bean burger, soy burger, meatless meat. . . . These terms so common in the twenty-first century appeared or were popularized during the Second World War. But, like the day care centers that sprang up during the war to enable women to work in munitions plants and other essential wartime industries, the fervent sense that a meatless burger could be the food of the future faded away. The post-war economy supported more traditional sources for protein and conventional roles for middle-class families.

Further Seventh Day Adventist developments

The Seventh Day Adventist economy—with companies producing the foods, advertisements in Seventh Day Adventist newspapers, and products available at Seventh Day Adventist food stores and found in hospitals—was hiding in plain sight. Their stores in large or small cities offered a non-meat version of many favorite family foods. Throughout the century they continued to develop meatless burgers.

In 1949, Loma Linda released the Vegemeat Burger (or Vegemeatburger—calling Lucille Ball). Ten years later, we can find Worthington Foods advertising vegetarian burgers. When, in 1968, Seventh Day Adventists Rosalie and Frank Hurd in their Ten Talents provided recipes for Almond-

Lentil Patties, Millet-Pumpkin Seed Patties, Hi-Protein Millet Patties, Walnut Oat Burgers, Soy-Millet Patties, Barley Burgers, and Sprouted Wheat Burgers, they began a publishing phenomenon.

The 1960s and the counterculture burger

Several aspects of the 1960s helped to create an expanding market for the veggie burger, including the environmental movement, awareness of world hunger, and the anti-war movement. The popularizing of yoga during the 1960s also helped. In 1962, Richard Hittleman in his *Be Young with Yoga* included the yogic case against flesh eating (while warning his readers they will be seen as food "faddists" or "crackpots").[20] *The Yoga Cook Book* by Edna Thompson, published in 1959 offered Hittleman's readers and other yoga followers a recipe for soy burgers.[21]

The home of the campus Free Speech Movement also helped popularize the veggie burger. A sandwich stand near the campus of the University of California, Berkeley offered the "Village Soyburger" in 1967.

In 1971, *Diet for a Small Planet* galvanized people to reconsider their meat-centric diet for environmental and human welfare reasons, and offered alternatives. Besides the bean burger mentioned above (p. 91), one could learn how to prepare garbanzo patties. Lappé's book was shortly followed by Edward Espé Brown *Tassajara Cooking*; Brown's recipe for a soy burger called for soybeans, rice, onions, carrot, celery, garlic, eggs, and wheat germ or oatmeal. A year after Brown's book appeared, The Farm—which pioneered cooking with soy and nutritional yeast—published a recipe for soy burgers.

Twenty years after *The Seven Year Itch* presented the soy burger as abnormal, the very mainstream newspapers, the *Christian Science Monitor* and *Wall Street Journal*, offered recipes for soy burgers and articles on bean burgers. (Prices for animal flesh prompted a search for alternatives.)[22]

Two books with considerable influence appeared in the mid-1970s: the 1975 *Book of Tofu: Food for Mankind* by William Shurtleff and Akiko Aoyagi (with recipes for okara burgers [okara is soybean pulp from making soy milk], soy burgers, and tofu burgers) and the 1976 *Laurel's Kitchen: A Handbook for Vegetarian Cookery and Nutrition*. The *Book of Tofu* introduced recipes for soy burgers by saying, "Now increasingly available at natural food stores, soy burgers are also easily prepared at home."[23]

One could prepare veggie burgers at home, or begin to find them in restaurants and available as a commercial product in stores other than Seventh Day Adventist-run stores, like the Soy Burger from East West Cookery or the Sunburger introduced by Nature's Oven and sold at seven restaurants around Fort Lauderdale. In 1976, a tofu burger was introduced at the University of Maine at Orono. By 1977, local restaurants caught on to the interest in

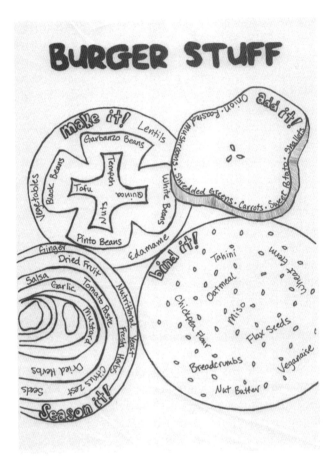

FIGURE 11 Elle Minter, "Burger Stuff."
Illustration © 2017 Elle Minter.

non-meat burgers. Uncle Munchie's in Indianapolis advertised in the *Indianapolis Star* before Thanksgiving promising "Complete dinners and sandwiches from Veggieburgers to steaks."[24]

The development of more and more veggie burgers prompted Marian Burros to declare in the *New York Times* in 1995, "This quintessential hippie food [the tofu burger] may be on its way to becoming the food of the masses." She rated thirty-four kinds of veggie burgers, judging as her favorites: Boca Burger, Green Giant Harvest Burger, and Morningstar Farms Meatless Patties made by Worthington Foods.[25]

Tempeh burgers

In 1981, three companies introduced tempeh burgers: White Wave, Pacific Tempeh, and North Coast Tempeh Co.; more soon followed—one of the most beloved (especially by me) was Tofurky's tempeh burger.

I asked Seth Tibbott, founder of Tofurky, about the beginnings of the tempeh burger. "The tempeh burger was actually a very historic burger. The first company to produce a tempeh burger that I remember was Pacific Tempeh in San Francisco, they made a tempeh burger that they deep fried. This was a revolutionary product, before Gardenburger, before many other burgers were available—a vacuum-packed refrigerated burger."

FIGURE 12 Move over Big Mac.
Courtesy: The Tofurky Company..

Ron Rosenbaum railed against the tempeh burger in *Esquire* in 1983,

> I'm sorry, I draw the line at tempeh. I had no qualms about tasting soy burgers, tofu burgers, lentil-walnut burgers, and sunflower-seed burgers, but I simply refuse to taste a tempeh burger. . . . Tempeh, if you must know, is soybeans fermented with a mold. Soyheads say that tempeh has all sorts of high quality-protein benefits you can't get even from the highly acclaimed soybean-curd tofu. It's the hot new item on the health food scene. I don't care. All I can

FIGURE 13 Super Burgers.
Courtesy: The Tofurky Company..

think of when I hear "tempeh" is those pallid squares of tofu floating in basins of dirty water in health food stores and developing mold. Yucch. I'm all for the health benefits of natural foods, but I have some aesthetic standards. . . . The idea here was to search for a health food alternative to the hamburger, something that tasted good on the sensual level and satisfied on the soulful level. . . . Do the substitutes offer that kind of satisfaction? Well, forget about tofu burgers. We're looking for hamburger alternatives, not hamburger helper. Tofu burgers are so bland, so ascetic, so utterly tasteless that they may be natural as hell but they taste like polyester.[26]

Well, I am glad he got that off his chest. But notice, as Tofurky's Seth Tibbott remarked when I read it to him, "Americans don't do the nuance thing well. He starts talking about tempeh, but quickly moves onto tofu. They are two different things."

Rosenbaum completely misunderstands the fermentation process for tempeh. And fermentation is back, big time in the twenty-first century so he also loses marks for lack of prescience! The tempeh burger is an artisanal burger, different from and more difficult to make than other burgers. In 1987, Tofurky came out with a revised upscale version of the tempeh burger that they called the Super Burger. With tempeh, brown rice, and wild rice, they were marinated in soy sauce, lemon juice, and garlic.

Seth described the process:

First, you have to grow the soybeans into tempeh. For efficiency we had muffin-like trays made. We put the inoculated beans in the cups, then we grow the tempeh in the shape of a burger, then we put them in a hot boiling soy sauce marinade and cook them and that gets flavor into them.

Cooking the beans, drying the beans, inoculating the beans, and growing the beans into tempeh . . . to make a palate of tempeh burgers takes two days. You are only able to produce a fraction of the number of burgers that Boca or Garden burger can produce.

The Boxed Mix

The Boxed Mix is actually a latecomer to the burgeoning veggie burger business. Advertisements for the "Sesame Burger Mix" from Fearn Soya Foods can be found in the *Vegetarian Times* as early as November 1977. Soon Fantastic Foods' "Nature's Burger Mix" joined the Sesame Burger Mix in the pages of *Vegetarian Times* (March 1979).

Other mixes followed: Tofu Burger Mix (Meatless) also from Fantastic Foods (1983)—"Just mash one pound of tofu and combine with our mix, shape into patties, and cook. In just minutes you will be enjoying delicious and nutritious tofu burgers." And Archer Daniel Midland joined the group with their 1986 Veggie Burger (Dry Mix with Textured Soy Protein Concentrate).

The simplicity of the product—add boiling water to the contents, shape into patties, and fry—worked for and against it. Some remember it with fondness; some were less enamored.

Scientific innovations create a new veggie burger

Soybean crushing converts soybeans into soy oil and soy meal. Words that will be common a hundred years later in reference to some veggie burgers made from soy—words like "extraction," "crush," and "solvent"—began to appear at the turn into the twentieth century.[27] In their definitive and exhaustive history of soybean crushing, the SoyInfo Center finds in 1908 in England "the first record of the soybean being crushed mainly for its oil and meal." At that time the oil went to soap and the soybean meal to farmed animals.

The common way for separating oil from soybeans was the expeller system using, for instance, hydraulic pressure. But in the early 1930s, Archer Daniels Midland acquired from Germany "a 150-ton-per-day capacity Hildebrandt continuous-flow, counter-current (U-tube) hexane solvent extractor." It used hexane as a solvent with the soybeans to separate the oil from the meal. Hexane solvent is distilled out of petroleum, with a low boiling point of 50 to 70 degrees centigrade. Once soybeans are cracked, heated, and flaked the soybeans "are soaked in a hexane bath to extract the oil. Then the oil and defatted flakes are each steamed to evaporate the hexane."[28]

The real break came in 1970, when [William] Atkinson patented a cheap and comparatively simple process for imparting "chew" to soybean flour by moistening it into a "plasticized" mass, bringing it to a high temperature, and rapidly forcing it through perforated dies into a chamber of lower temperature and pressure. The result is a neutral-tasting granular material of any desired size and shape, depending on the dies, which contains about five percent moisture. When these granules are mixed with water, they retain their structural integrity, and in feel and texture resemble moist bits of hamburger.[29]

In 1975, the Food and Drug Administration changed its policy regarding soy protein: it no longer required the word "imitation" to be used on labels containing soy protein, as long as these products are nutritionally equivalent to the real thing.[30]

It is possible that small amounts of hexane end up in veggie meats. One report asserts this is dangerous to human health; many scientists disagree with that claim, arguing that scientific studies have found "no evidence to substantiate any risk or danger to consumer health when foods containing trace residual concentrations of hexane are ingested."[31]

In 1994, the Subway chain of sandwiches began to offer Boca Burgers. One small chain, Back Yard Burgers, with about 100 restaurants in seventeen states, started selling Gardenburger meatless patties on its menu around 2000. In 2002, Burger King became the first major US fast food chain to put a veggie burger on its menu, at more than 8,000 outlets nationwide. McDonald's tried a veggie burger in 2004 on the West Coast and to the disappointment of many, abandoned it. Veggie burgers can be found in many other chains and McDonalds is now testing one.

The *Smithsonian* missed the veggie burger's beginnings by about eighty years. They missed other developments, too, such as the appearance of the Vital burger, the Sizzle burger, the Love burger, all the DIY burgers, other box mixes, the

Seventh Day Adventists, the Second World War innovations, and restaurants' individual burgers.

Though much of its history is submerged, the veggie burger evolved side by side with the hamburger throughout the twentieth century. Do we measure its cultural diffusion through its commercial availability? Its domestic role via recipes? Its appearance as a menu item in restaurants? When mainstream media took notice of it? Or, as did the *Smithsonian*, when it appears in a box?

Like the veggie burger itself, the answer is a mixture of these ingredients. Recipes affirmed the legitimacy of veggie burgers, especially when appearing in successful books like *Diet for a Small Planet* (more than 3 million copies were sold), and reiterated in recipe book after recipe book in the 1970s. Expanding availability when eating out helped to begin the process of normalizing the veggie burger. And those boxes? They allowed for quick preparation at home.

Its latest innovation is the jackfruit, from a nutrient-packed fruit cultivated in India for millennia; it has become a texture-rich burger ingredient.[32] Will the hamburger prevail against the largest fruit grown on the earth, resistant to pests and droughts? "Its nutritional credentials are also impressive: researchers have suggested it could replace wheat, corn and other staple crops that may come under threat because of climate change."[33]

The 2001 film *Scotland, Pa.* is a retelling of *Macbeth* set amid a pseudo-McDonald's hamburger restaurant. One of the main characters is a vegetarian cop named McDuff investigating a series of unfortunate occurrences. At the end of the movie, he opens a vegetarian restaurant in the former fast food joint under the banner "Home of the Veggie Burger." On opening day, the parking lot is empty.

Scotland, Pa. suggests that a veggie burger stand is not going to disrupt the hamburger business any time soon. Filmed close to twenty years ago, it did not anticipate the arrival of a new kind of burger.

7 MOON SHOT BURGER

In 2016, Eric Schmidt, the executive chairman of Alphabet (Google's parent company), identified the six most important contemporary game-changing technologies or "moon shots." Google's definition of a moon shot is

a project or proposal that

1   addresses a huge problem

2   proposes a radical solution

3   uses breakthrough technology.[1]

Schmidt listed plant-based meat first in his list of moon shots. He argued that "replacing livestock with growing and harvesting plants could reduce greenhouse gas emissions and fight climate change."[2]

One food writer deemed the work on plant-based meat as "the Manhattan Project of food."[3] Beyond Meat dubbed the development of the Beast Burger—one of its early plant-based meat burgers—"the Manhattan Beach Project."[4]

These metaphors evoke the ambitious, aspirational, and transformational nature of plant-based meat technologies. The founder of another of the companies, biochemist Pat Brown of Impossible Foods, described their goal as eliminating "the middle cow."[5]

During a 2009 sabbatical from Stanford University, Brown asked himself, "With a completely blank slate, what's the most important problem I can have an impact on?" His answer was climate change. He knew that by 2050, nine billion people would live on the planet. With a rising middle class throughout the world, diets are shifting to focus more on dairy and meat. Animal agriculture already requires 30 percent of ice-free land. Anticipating increased resource demand on fresh water and land, as well as increased carbon emissions, Brown asked himself, "People love meat, but does it have to be from animals? And if it isn't from animals, wouldn't they be just as happy?" He realized the answer did not require any top-down intervention from the government; he needed to make products that competed sustainably with current products. In the past, "every single burger happened to be made from a cow but the cow is never going to get better at making meat. It was not optimized for beef. It did not evolve to be eaten."

Plant-based meat does not target vegetarian or vegan consumers. The companies at the forefront of developing this alternative meat, some based in the tech innovation sector, are using food technology including synthetic biology to create burgers for meat eaters. Other companies are exploring tissue engineering to create "clean meat." These are radical solutions to the problem of the environmentally damaging $74 billion beef industry. The burger Pat Brown's team created uses 95 percent less land than cows, 74 percent less water, and creates 87 percent fewer greenhouse gas emissions. In addition, Brown points out this moon shot food will replace slaughterhouse jobs that are dangerous and low paying with better paying, safer jobs.

Another company, Beyond Meat, identifies the problems it addresses in four signs at its El Segundo, California headquarters: improve animal welfare, address global resource constraints, improve human health, and positively impact climate change with plant-based meat. When I visited the company in March 2017, its founder Ethan Brown pointed to the signs: "We are solving four problems with one solution: plant-based meat."

The largest US meat processor, Tyson Foods, launched a $150 million venture capital fund focused on sustainable food solutions, specifically alternative proteins. Tyson New Ventures LLC invested an unknown amount to gain a 5-percent ownership stake in Beyond Meat.[6]

Because hamburgers function both as icon and one of the main forms in which cows are consumed, the companies often begin by developing a burger. Pat Brown of Impossible Foods likened its burger to a "gateway drug" that shows that "delicious meat doesn't have to come from an animal." I think of these burgers as "moon shot burgers."

I met both Ethan and Pat (they are not related) in early 2017 when I headed to California to go into the belly of this new and fast-moving industry and sample a taste of the future.

Impossible Foods

I arrived at the headquarters of Impossible Foods in the heart of Silicon Valley drenched from the rainstorms hitting California in February 2017. Inside, along with a group of international and national journalists, we handed over our raincoats and umbrellas and donned lab coats and hairnets for a tour of a laboratory filled with hamburger smells.

When Pat Brown founded Impossible Foods, he assembled a team of molecular biologists, biochemists, and physicists to determine "What are the key components in the hamburger that makes it iconic?" "What are the molecules that make beef so delicious?" "How does real meat look, cook, and taste?" and "Which plants are necessary for the sensory experience we associate with hamburgers?"

Like forensic laboratories, Impossible Foods used gas chromatography, among other technologies, to analyze a small piece of ground cow flesh and separate its molecules for individual analysis. They narrowed the hamburger down to five main components:

1 *Texture.* Muscle (tissue) provides chew down texture. "Texture Sensory Research" in the lab kitchen determined the plants that act in the same way as

meat. For the Impossible Burger, they achieved that chew down texture with wheat protein (chewy) and potato protein (binds water well in the transition to cooking).

2 *Flavor.* Part of what drives meat's flavor is *heme protein*; it is a molecule that is red itself and bound to iron. Heme protein is in all forms of life; in legumes it is called *leghemoglobin*. How to get the heme protein in plants? Through fermentation by yeast, like the process for producing beer. Our tour took us past vast vats fermenting the yeast. The heme is then removed from the yeast by breaking open yeast cells, filtering to remove yeast solids, and then concentrating it down by removing the water; this becomes concentrated heme product—in a sense, plant-based blood.

It is the first time synthetic biology has been used in the production of any burger, vegetarian or otherwise. But while GMO modifies the yeast, the yeast itself is extracted out of the final product.

3 *Nutrients.* Amino acids, with a little bit of sugar, and vitamins.

4 *Carbohydrates compound.* A Japanese yam, Konja, is the main ingredient.

5 *Fat tissue.* Fat tissue allows for cohesion, traps aromas, and releases on cooking. Impossible Foods uses

coconut oil. The sensory experience Impossible Foods seeks to match is that 80 percent lean, 20 percent fat ration of the classic hamburger, but they achieve that experience with less fat.

At the Impossible Foods cooking demonstration, I positioned myself near the grill. The burgers performed unlike any veggie burger in my experience. As they heated up, they began to sizzle—not just fry but to really sizzle—and turn a bright rosy-pink color. Then the burgers browned, emitting familiar hamburger aromas until a spatula delivered each of them to buns. All around me, journalists chowed down on

FIGURE 14 The foods that make up an Impossible Burger, and in the back, on the right, the Impossible Burger before grilling, and on left, ready to be eaten.

Photograph by Eric Day for the Good Food Institute. February 7, 2017 at Impossible Foods, Redwood City, California.

the burgers. Before I knew it, I devoured the scrumptious burger. If etiquette allowed, I would have asked for another.

In 2015, Impossible Foods received an offer for purchase from Google. Brown turned the $200- to $300-million offer down. He explained, "The company is defined by a mission that—no matter how much someone who wants to acquire the company may say they believe in it—no one believes in it with the commitment that we do, and we're not going to put it at risk."[7] Their moon shot mission continues.

Beyond Meat

In El Segundo, California, the home of Beyond Meat, one can see their Research and Development "steer." It is an extruder, about the dimensions of a large steer, and like a steer it transforms plant material into "fibrous bundles of protein."[8]

Founder Ethan Brown suggests we should think about meat in terms of composition and not whether It is from an animal. Plant-based meat supplanting animal meat? He says It is like the cell phone displacing the landline. He told the *San Francisco Chronicle,* "I was struck by the idea that we've innovated and removed bottlenecks in every part of industry but not in agriculture. . . . We've always tried to make the animal more efficient, and there's a biological limit to that."[9]

We toured their laboratory, meeting scientists, many of whom came from the field of medicine now working to prevent some of the diseases they have seen (heart disease, diabetes, high cholesterol) that are linked to animal protein consumption.

The Beyond Burger contains pea protein. (Brown envisions a time when we go to the meat department and ask ourselves, "Do I want lentil protein today? Or pea? Or soy?") The pea protein is separated in water, then run through a process of heating, cooling, and pressure to realign it to take on the fibrous texture of muscle. Brown compared it to the way diamonds are formed under pressure; they are stitching together protein to be the texture of animal flesh. Brown said, "At the end of the day, what we are trying to do is getting meat to people. We can assemble meat in the same architecture." The next step is adding aroma and taste.

In the Beyond Meat kitchen an animal-free burger acted like a hamburger, sizzling and turning color, caramelizing through the Maillard reaction. Named for the chemist who described it in 1912, this chemical reaction between amino acids and sugars browns the flesh of the hamburger during cooking. The reaction contributes to the experience of eating a hamburger, not so much because of the change in color but through the flavors and aromas released during the browning.[10]

The Beyond Burger contains beet and annatto extracts in it for color. But it also needed fat to be distributed throughout the patty without the help of the ligaments in animal meat. Coconut oil, which is firm when cold but melts during cooking, accounted in part for the Maillard reaction. The smell and sight of the burger cooking produced cognitive dissonance, only further intensified with the first bite. Then I took another.

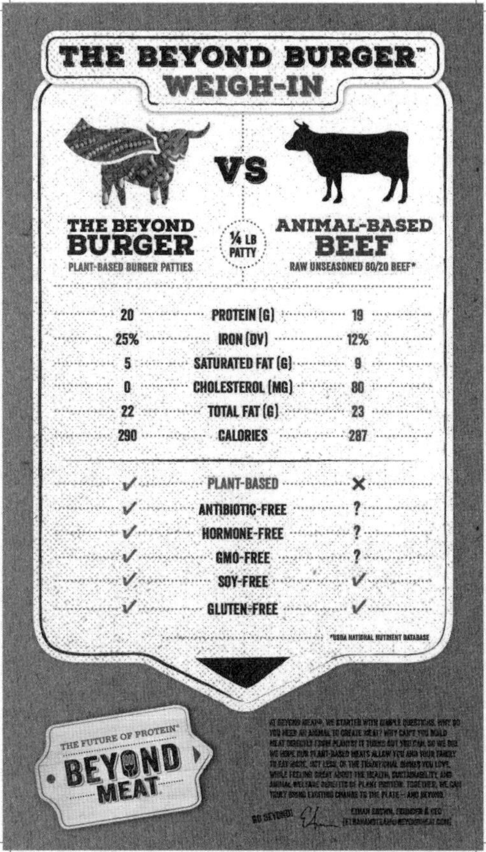

FIGURE 15 "Beyond Burger Weigh In."

Courtesy Beyond Foods.

The Beyond Burger is the first plant-based burger sold in the meat departments of Whole Foods and Safeway grocery stores. When it first debuted in a Whole Foods, the supplies could not keep up with demand. Brown also anticipates a day when ordering the Beyond Burger at McDonald's or In-N-Out Burger would be unremarkable.

The clean meat burger

The clean meat burger is not a plant-based burger, but it shares the goal of eliminating meat taken directly from dead animals. "Clean meat" is real meat grown in a laboratory from animal cells without animal slaughter. Though sometimes called *cultured* or *in vitro* meat, its advocates argue that the term *clean meat*, akin to *clean energy*, is more accurate for meat grown through cellular agriculture "in that it immediately communicates important aspects of the technology—both the environmental benefits and the decrease in food-borne pathogens and drug residues."[11] By detaching meat production from the slaughter process, the contamination that comes from fecal material or the guts will be avoided.

Unlike the Impossible Burger and the Beyond Burger, the clean meat burger is not available for sale to consumers as of this writing. The first clean meat hamburger was eaten in London on August 5, 2013, brought there by Mark Post from Maastricht University. The burger cost close to $300,000.

New Harvest, the not-for-profit supporting breakthroughs in cellular agriculture, explained:

> It cost this much because the project took place at laboratory scale. The technicians making the burger did so by producing very small strands of beef in standard tissue culture flasks, and repeating this work several thousands of times. The price of the burger was so high because it included the salaries of skilled technicians doing very time-consuming work and consuming expensive laboratory supplies.[12]

The researchers needed to figure out how to help the muscle fibers mature and how to grow a large number of muscle cells. They used fetal bovine serum at first, but "by the end of the production of the burger, the muscle strands were grown in media with zero fetal bovine serum."[13] As the cells grow, forming muscle tissue, "they are attached to a biodegradable scaffold, just as vines wrap around a trellis."[14]

Post, a vascular biologist and surgeon with a doctorate in pulmonary pharmacology, works with MosaMeat to develop a clean meat hamburger. He told Michael Specter of the *New Yorker*:

> We have an opportunity to reverse the terribly damaging impact that eating animals has had on our lives and on this planet. . . . The goal is to take the meat from one

animal and create the volume previously provided by a million animals.[15]

In the United States, CEO and cofounder of Memphis Meats, Dr. Uma Valeti, a cardiologist, is working toward a clean meat hamburger and other clean meats. When he worked at the Mayo Clinic, he saw how muscle regenerated with heart attack victims. He asked himself, "Why can't we do the same process and method to grow meat?" He became involved with New Harvest, and saw a significant amount of interest globally in the questions, "Can we do this better? Can we do a more sustainable meat production method or techniques?"

He decided to assemble a team. His cofounder, Nicholas Genovese, is an expert in skeletal muscle biology, and Memphis Meats began its work:

> Instead of growing a full animal over 12 to 24 months and then slaughtering it, . . . we are growing the same meat from the fundamental building blocks of life, which are the meat cells. We identify the best meat cells possible whether from a cow or a pig, . . . and from these cells we identify those that are capable of self-renewing themselves, and we cultivate them in a very safe and clean environment, so that they can grow just like a small plant grows into a larger plant, using nutrients, amino acids, peptides, minerals, vitamins, oxygen, sugars, and once we get the meat to a consistency we like for the product, we harvest the meat.

Making Clean Meat

The process of growing meat in a lab may be hard to imagine. Here is how clean meat is made, from lab to plate.

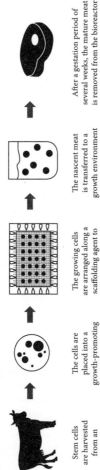

Stem cells are harvested from an animal.

The cells are placed into a growth-promoting liquid.

The growing cells are arranged along a scaffolding agent to give them structure.

The nascent meat is transferred to a growth environment called a bioreactor.

After a gestation period of several weeks, the mature meat is removed from the bioreactor and packaged for consumption.

FIGURE 16 This infographic was republished with permission from *VegNews* magazine, America's premier vegan lifestyle publication.

Their first product, a meatball, debuted in 2016. In March 2017 they revealed a clean meat chicken. Valeti believes that "in 20 years, a majority of meat sold in stores will be cultured";[16] the public will have parted from inherently inefficient meat production techniques. "It takes about 23 calories of grain to make one calorie of beef. The process we are modeling out right now, takes about three calories of energy input to make one calorie of beef."

Memphis Meats needs the ability to scale up so that they can manufacture clean meat in large quantities.[17] Valeti says funding is their biggest hurdle. MosaMeats projects selling its clean meat hamburgers for $10 a patty by 2020, and after that, at a cost competitive with cheap hamburger. Valeti sees Memphis Meats using the same distribution system and packaging as the current meat industry. Whether the clean meat burger will catch up with the moon shot burger, and whether it will be able to shed its reliance on sourcing meat from dead animals, will only be known down the road.

Challenges to the development of the moon shot burger

A moon shot is not a guaranteed thing. In specific, the moon shot burger faces several challenges.

1 *Scale.* As this book went to press, the companies were expanding their production capabilities, but were still

in the early stages to meet their most ambitious goals. In March 2017, Impossible Foods opened a plant in Oakland, California, capable of monthly production of at least one million pounds of food.[18] Impossible Foods is looking to "scale up" production by more than 100-fold. Ethan Brown expects to be able to undercut beef by 2022, as Beyond Meat increases the scale of production because the cost of ingredients, and their product, will decrease.[19] By the middle of 2017, it was available in Kroger, Wegmans, and Safeway.

2   *Funding.* To scale up, funding is needed. Valeti says funding is their biggest hurdle. UBS, Viking Global Investors, Microsoft cofounder Bill Gates, and Horizons Ventures have invested in Impossible Foods. As noted, Tyson invested in Beyond Meat. New Crop Capital, formed to provide "early-stage investments to companies that develop cultured and plant-based meat, dairy, and egg products, as well as service companies that facilitate the promotion and sale of such products," offers investments from $50,000 to $1 million to companies.[20]

3   *Myths about food and technology.* Some people say about the association of Silicon Valley with the new burgers, "We don't want to have technology associated with our hamburger." The idea that technology is not involved in the production of the hamburger is

a belief born of nostalgia married to ignorance and custom. The hamburger exists because of modernist technologies, from the barbed wire to the stun gun. The antibiotics and hormones used to promote growth and suppress diseases in animals were developed by technology. The cheeseburger relies on rennet in cow's milk-based cheeses; most rennet is produced by synthetic biology. The yeast used to produce the heme for the Impossible Burger is only used in the production; it is then recycled, not consumed.

4   *Because of the gendered nature of meat consumption, marketing plant-based meat to men poses a challenge.*[21] Of the problem, Ethan Brown said, "meat has a masculine bent to it," one cannot "sell it the same way they sell lettuce."[22]

5   *Pricing.* The moon shot burgers are not yet competitive in price with hamburgers; they do not benefit from the federal subsidies that continue to protect animal agriculture.

Plant-based meat burgers have only recently entered the market. Different market strategies for companies unveiling their products indicate how they wish consumers to experience their foods. The folks at Impossible Foods are looking to replace all meat and dairy starting with restaurants. They launched their product on July 26, 2016 at Momofuku

Nishi in New York; after it debuted, the "lunch business skyrocketed at Nishi, which was notable, since it happened after a series of negative reviews."[23] In 2017, the Impossible Burger could be found in several high-end restaurants, as well as Bare Burger, Hopdoddy, Burgatory, Umami Burger, and numerous other restaurants. Beyond Meat continues to eye the meat departments of grocery stores as the site for its products, but is also found in Alamo Drafthouses and other restaurants. In September 2017, it greatly expanded its reach as it joined up with the food service company Sysco, which supplies food to fast-food chains, hotels, and cafeterias in hospitals and schools.

Bruce Friedrich, the executive director of the Good Food Institute and one of the trustees of New Crop Capital, believes the moon shot burger will prevail. "People eat meat despite how it is produced, not because of how it is produced. People make their food decisions based on taste, price, and convenience. Once you take care of taste and price, convenience will take care of itself." After all, that is how the hamburger evolved. Or as Rowan Jacobsen observes, "Culture is a lump of flesh wrapped in dough. If you want to save the world, you'd better make it convenient."[24] And then place it between a bun.

FIGURE 17 Suzy González, "Slippage".

Illustration © 2017, Suzy González.

AFTERWORD: *SLIPPAGE*

"Lord of the Fries" is the first food place one espies upon arriving in Melbourne by train. It is across the street from the station, anchoring the corner. Trained in low expectations—the kind that vegans carry along with their bags—I did not consider the entire menu, but ordered their fries. Later, at the hotel a few blocks away I thought about it and remembered a menu reference to gravy that was vegan. I realized with a start the whole thing appeared to be one thing, a fast food stand, but was another: a *vegetarian* fast food stand. The burgers appeared to be one thing but were another or they were both, conventional burger and liberated burger.

From the moment the hamburger, grilled and sizzling, flopped onto a bun and was handed to a customer it began to change—and not just by the question of whether it was accompanied by lettuce, ketchup, or tomato. The first definition of a hamburger might have been "a patty made of beef between buns." But then Walter Anderson added fried onions in 1916. In the Depression, crackers supplemented the meat; in the Second World War, soy protein extended it. Innovation continued to work on the hamburger, and soon kimchi, avocado, and sundried tomatoes replaced the lettuce, tomatoes, and onions—condiments displaced by accouterments. The bun's embrace of the patty was complicated as layers of additions were introduced.

It was sized up, double, triple, big boys, big macs, bigger boys, and on and on and on. (Well, not the last one). By its elaborations the burger becomes not fixed but multiple.

The burger's identity has always been in motion, and not just because people can walk and eat a burger at the same time. Has not the hamburger always contained, not just change, but an aspect of deception within it? Named for a city that did not originate it, a form and method of presenting flesh that often relied on disguise (flesh past its prime, pink slime), in the twenty-first century it achieved the apotheosis of not being what it is presented to be, the burger with everything but the meat.

I am not the only one who comes to a fast food stand with expectations. There are those who think "I don't want to give up my hamburger." The second part of the thought is usually unstated, "And I don't have to!" But what if they have simultaneously given up their burger as they conceive of it, but not given up their burger? What if, like me, they do not catch on to the place and order the double cheeseburger (no longer on the menu at Lord of the Fries)? Is the unmarked, slaughterless burger our future?

Before an interview with a *New York Times* reporter, I checked out some of his earlier writings. One sentence stood out, "My ongoing fondness for cheeseburgers."[1]

When he interviewed me,[2] I mentioned his cheeseburger habit and suggested that he might want to check out the new developments in veggie burgers. He was game. He chowed down on a variety of veggie burgers and interviewed chefs who created new versions. "If you're going to do a veggie burger, it should have that richness and mouth feel and overall texture. When you pick it up, it should eat like a burger," Josh Capon of SoHo's Burger & Barrel told him.[3] He also visited the home of a veggie burger cookbook author. Lukas Volger made three burgers for Jeff Gordinier: one with mushrooms and barley, another with tofu and chard, and one a touch-of-peanut Thai-style rendition with carrots. Volger explained to Gordinier—mid-bite into one of Volger's creations—that veggie burgers were not "just an approximation of a meat burger," (imagine a few more bites here), "It's an expression of a vegetable."[4]

Cookbook authors of titles like *Wicked Good Burgers: Fearless Recipes and Uncompromising Techniques for the Ultimate Patty* include veggie burgers with the acknowledgment that non-vegans will like them too: "After a bit of trial and error (we admit it; it wasn't easy), we created a completely vegan burger that has the great meaty texture everyone loves about burgers; and it's delicious. We bet your carnivorous friends will enjoy them as much as those who never touch the animal stuff."[5]

When Ronald McDonald, a fictional factotum, acknowledges eating "a wide variety of all-vegetable 'garden burgers' in my time," the slippage of the hamburger achieved a new ironic moment, even before one of Ronald's recipe added tofu to hamburger meat.[6]

In Bill Watterson's *Calvin and Hobbes* cartoon for October 22, 1993, the precocious Calvin is shown chewing his first bite of a hamburger. Mouth full and cheeks bulging he asks, "Is hamburger meat made out of people from Hamburg?"

"Of course not!" his mother replies, just about to take her first bite. "It's ground beef."

Calvin stares at his hamburger. "I'm eating a cow?"

"Right," his mother says.

He thrusts the hamburger off the plate, turns his face aside, and exclaims, "I don't think I can finish this!"

In 1973, I experienced a Calvin-like moment though I did not need to be disabused of the notion that hamburger meat might be from people. (As usual, Watterson suggests the ironic essence of Calvin: cannibalism seemed a little more acceptable to him than eating a cow.) Like the women Billy Ingram described, my mother would ask for her animal flesh to be ground by the local butcher. As her children grew from childhood to teenager, we would be sent uptown to ask the proprietor to take some ground chuck and grind it as we waited. That is what I did in 1973, the night my pony was killed when some teens were target shooting near the pasture where he sheltered. My father suggested we have hamburgers and, still stunned from confronting the dead body of my beloved pony, I walked uptown to ask Jim to grind some chuck for hamburger.

Once home, as I bit into the cooked hamburger, the trauma of a pony dying hours earlier prompted images of dead bodies. "I am eating a dead cow," I thought, as I put down the hamburger.

When I think about my last hamburger, it is not the one I bit into the night my pony was killed. In 1978, en route to Australia on a Rotary Graduate Fellowship, I stopped for a visit with Chellis Glendinning (a future ecopsychologist and author of *My Name is Chellis and I Am in Recovery from Western Civilization*). One night, I dreamed I was in a fast-food restaurant where, no matter how many times I refused a cheeseburger being handed to me by an employee, I was once again handed a cheeseburger. I awoke crying. I reported the dream to Chellis and she asked, "What are you giving yourself that you don't want?" Musing on Chellis's apposite question as my bus returned over the Golden Gate Bridge to continue my trip, I realized it was the trip itself. It was the trip that I did not want. I gave up the fellowship, handed in a round-the-world airplane ticket, and returned to western New York where I had fallen in love and become involved in rural social justice activism.

Are we ever *just* eating? We are consuming interspecies history, environmental history, national history, and gender politics. A hamburger is never just a hamburger, even in a dream. What are we giving ourselves that we do not want?

One caveat about discussions of consumer choice: Focusing only on the individual as a consumer separates us from some larger determining factors that influenced the success of the hamburger: policy decisions, systemic issues, and moral concerns that could be more accurate and productive for discussion.[7] In the United States, federal subsidies to the cow business and other institutionalized supports suppress the true costs of the hamburger. The Worldwatch Institute Report on Progress Toward a Sustainable Society says, "All told, the price of meat might double or triple if the full ecological costs—including fossil fuel use, ground-water depletion, agricultural-chemical pollution, and methane and ammonia emissions—were included in the bill."[8] The question also must be "What are we being given by others that we do not want?"

At the end of *The Founder*, Director John Lee Hancock's movie on Ray Kroc, a statistic is offered: McDonald's daily feeds 1 percent of the population of the world. But it is not the hamburger that is necessarily feeding that 1 percent. (Not to be confused with Wall Street's 1 Percent.) McDonald's added salads and wraps and fish on Fridays, then fish every day. In Russia, they added potato wedges, cabbage pie, and cherry pie. They increased their profits when they started serving Egg McMuffins all day long. McDonald's embraced the veggie burger in other countries, especially India.

As analog gave way to digital, new iterations of food companies appear. Coca-Cola buys Dasani water; it is in the consumable liquids business. Dean Foods, a dairy company, buys White Wave, a leader in producing soy milk. It is in the generic milk, not the dairy, business.

Tyson Foods, the country's largest flesh processor, buys a 5-percent stake in Beyond Meat, maker of a non-meat burger. Pinnacle Foods, maker of "Hungry Man," bought Gardein, a plant-based protein series of products. Maple Leaf Farms in Canada bought Light Life. They are diversifying their protein source to get ahead of (or catch up with) the consumer.

Burger chains like Burger King add veggie burgers, becoming purveyors of burgers, not *ham*burgers.

Has not the hamburger always been a sign of instability, around which superstructures (golden arches, castle turrets) are built in attempts to stabilize it, mythologize it? In *Reification, or The Anxiety of Late Capitalism*, Timothy Bewes suggests that reification contains within it its own resistance. Does the hamburger, that ultimate symbol of reification—thingifying living beings by shaping their dead bodies into meat—contain the making of its own dissolution/disappearance within it? And not only because dead bodies decay? Is the hamburger a modernist aberration, albeit a very successful one, in the long tradition of shaping protein food items into single-portion meals? If so, what is replacing it?

The everyday object of burgerness.

The non-meat burger is no longer the uncanny, the unbelievable, the crank's food, the chewy cardboard mocked by food reviewers. Dr. Aaron M. Altschul, head of the nutrition program at Georgetown University School of Medicine, was quoted in 1973 saying, "The ability to produce texture out of soy flour will probably rank with the invention of bread as one of the truly great inventions of food."[9] Perhaps he will yet be proven right.

Will the non-meat burger bring about "the end of meat as we know it"?[10] Certainly, food critics are no longer approaching "burgerness" with confusion or fear or revilement. Instead, they are voting vegan burgers the top burger. *Gentlemen's Quarterly* granted Superiority Burger's vegan burger the status of top burger of the year in 2015 with a headline heralding "The Best Burger of the Year Has No Meat in It."[11] Superiority Burger's chef Brooks Headley talked to the *Wall Street Journal* about making his award-winning burger. "'I don't need something indistinguishable from meat in order to feel like I'm eating a hamburger,' said Mr. Headley. 'The act of eating a burger is so iconic and so American, and it's not just about the patty. It's the squish of the bun and the crunch of the lettuce and the tang of the ketchup—there's something primally satisfying in all that.'"[12]

Despite its continuing hold on the fast food market, is the hamburger more like another of Claes Oldenberg's sculptures, the typewriter eraser, soon to be displaced by technological advances? At the end of our tour of Impossible Foods, I mentioned to the founder Pat Brown that I was working on a book on the cultural history of the burger. He replied, "The cultural *prehistory* of the burger, you mean." Time will tell whether that modernist icon and legacy of colonialism, the hamburger, finds its place in the bun superseded.

ACKNOWLEDGMENTS

Forrest Girod Nearing was the son of Jane Girod Nearing. Jane is the research librarian who has ferreted out books, articles, and newspaper advertisements for me, not just for this book, but earlier ones. After her son's tragic death in 2016, Jane and I perhaps, in some small way, created a space in which Forrest's spirit could reside as we investigated possible reference sources. Knowing my excitement over old sources, Jane found and obtained for me information that greatly enhanced the book's depth. I realized we were knitting Forest's memory into the book through our interactions and I want explicitly to acknowledge that.

Jane is on staff at my local library, a wonderful resource filled with caring people—a reminder of all that makes a library the important civic resource it is. I want to thank, as well, Susan Allison, the executive director, and all the staff who patiently helped me check out Interlibrary Loan books.

In addition, many people have been helpful as I worked on *Burger*: First, Haaris Naqvi, my editor at Bloomsbury, and the coeditors of the Object Lessons series, Chris Schaberg and Ian Bogost. Support in my research and work came from people I greatly admire for their own work, including Bill Shurtleff, Christopher Schlottmann, Mark Hawthorne, lauren Ornelas, Laura Wright, Roger Yates, Silke Feltz, Vasile Stănescu, Gwendolyn L. Carroll, and Seth Tibbott.

Thanks to the many people who answered my survey on veggie burgers and Emma Patterson for helping me think about them! And to Facebook friends who brainstormed popular culture references to the veggie burger.

The folk at the Good Food Institute, specifically Bruce Friedrich, Emily Byrd, Eric Wells, and Toube Benedetto helped me understand the moon shot burger and visit companies making them. Kirsta Hackmeier of the Humane Society helped me with statistics and definitions. I appreciated my interview time with Todd and Jody Boyman.

Thanks to Pat Brown and his team at Impossible Foods and Ethan Brown and his team at Beyond Meat for introducing me to their product and their company's commitments. As I researched for "Burger," thanks to nephews Chris Fry and spouse Kim Harley, and Ben Fry and spouse Lindsay, for hospitality. Thanks to Jeff Gordinier for our conversation.

During the final lap before the deadline, Punk Rawk Labs sent their plant-based cheese for sustenance and Christina Nakhoda and Carol Mai brought food. Mmm. Thanks! As usual, sisters Jane and Nancy helped; as did spouse Bruce Buchanan, who responds with loving patience to my relentlessness; he also tested burgers with me. The condiments to marriage, perhaps!

For help with images I appreciate the assistance of Alessandra Pozzati of the Ugo Mulas Archives, Mark Hess, David Bressler of *New York* magazine, Soraya Membreno of Bitch Media, Seth Tibbott of Tofurky, Bill Shurtleff of the SoyInfo Center, Ethan Brown and Anne Marie McDermott of Beyond Meat, Jasmin Singer of *VegNews* magazine, xkcd.com, Benjamin Buchanan, the artists Jill Jones, Suzy Gonzalez, Patricia Denys, and Elle Minter and photographers Eric Day, Roger Yates, and Micha Warren. Nods to Jan Muir for "Move Over Big Mac," and the anonymous artist of the original "McLibel" pamphlet.

LIST OF ILLUSTRATIONS

NOTES

Chapter 1

1 David Gerard Hogan, *Selling 'em by the Sack: White Castle and the Creation of American Food* (New York and London: New York University Press, 1997), 175.

2 William Shurtleff and Akiko Aoyagi, *History of Meat Alternatives (965 CE to 2014)* (Lafayette, CA: Soyinfo Center, 2014), #2716, 991, quoting *Western Livestock Journal* (Denver, Colorado) June 27, 1994; future references will be "HMA" followed by item number.

3 Elisabeth Rozin, *The Primal Cheeseburger* (New York: Penguin Books, 1994).

4 "Food: The Burger that Conquered the Country," *Time*, September 17, 1973, http://content.time.com/time/subscriber/article/0,33009,907911-10,00.html (Accessed February 28, 2017).

5 Bobby Flay, *Bobby Flay's Burgers, Fries & Shakes* (New York: Clarkson Potter, 2009), 11.

6 John Ayto, *The Diner's Dictionary* (Oxford and New York: Oxford University Press, 1993), 158.

7 Alan Davidson, *The Oxford Companion to Food* (Oxford and New York: Oxford University Press, 1999), 182.

8 Quoted in Evan Jones, *American Food: The Gastronomic* Story (New York: E. P. Dutton and Co., Inc., 1975), 137.

9 Erik Piepenburgaug, "The Veggie Burger's Ascent," *New York Times*, August 30, 2016, https://www.nytimes.com/2016/08/31/dining/veggie-burgers.html?_r=0 (Accessed January 17, 2017).

10 *Oxford Companion to Food*, 369.

Chapter 2

1 Hannah Velten, *Cow* (London: Reaktion Books, 2007), 22.

2 Obituary for Frank Menches, *New York Times*, October 5, 1951. https://timesmachine.nytimes.com/timesmachine/1951/10/05/issue.html?action=clickandcontentCollection=Archivesandmodule=LedeAssetandregion=ArchiveBodyandpgtype=article. (Accessed January 17, 2017).

3 Wayne Caldwell Neely, *The Agricultural Fair* (New York: Columbia University Press, 1935), 104.

4 Neely, *The Agricultural Fair*, 14.

5 http://www.louislunch.com/history.php (Accessed February 14, 2017).

6 Michael Knight, "Burger 'Birthplace' Faces Bulldozer," *New York Times*, January 12, 1974, 35, http://www.nytimes.com/1974/01/12/archives/burger-birthplace-faces-bulldozer-a-landmark-since-1967.html?_r=0 (Accessed February 28, 2017).

7 Gary Cartwright, "The World's First Hamburger Was Served in Athens, Texas, No Matter What Mr. Cutlets Says," *Texas Monthly*, August 2009, http://www.texasmonthly.com/food/the-worlds-first-hamburger/ (Accessed February 28, 2017).

8   http://www.webersoftulsa.com/webers_story.asp (Accessed
    February 14, 2017).

9   Upton Sinclair, *The Jungle* (New York: New American Library,
    1973), 162.

10 Quoted in Robert B. Downs, afterword to *The Jungle*, 346.

11 Edgar W. Ingram, Sr., *All This from a 5-Cent Hamburger!:
    The Story of the White Castle System* (New York: Newcomen
    Society in North America, 1964), 10.

12 This summary draws on Hogan, *Selling 'em by the Sack.*

13 Daniel Marcus, *Happy Days and Wonder Years: The Fifties
    and the Sixties in Contemporary Politics* (New Brunswick, NJ:
    Rutgers University Press), 177.

14 Marcus, *Happy Days and Wonder Years*, 181.

15 Eric B. Ross, "Patterns of Diet and Forces of Production: An
    Economic and Ecological History of the Ascendancy of Beef in
    the United States Diet," in *Beyond the Myths of Culture: Essay
    in Cultural Materialism*, ed. Eric Ross (New York: Academic
    Press, 1980), 213.

16 Ross, "Patterns," 213.

17 Andrew Smith, *Hamburger: A Global History* (London:
    Reaktion Books, 2008), 44.

18 John F. Love, *McDonald's: Behind the Arches* (Toronto: Bantam
    Books, 1986), 5.

19 Mimi Sheraton, "The Burger That's Eating New York,"
    New York magazine, August 19, 1974, 34, 35.

20 Quoted in Evan Jones, *American Food: The Gastronomic Story*
    (New York: Dutton, 1975), 135.

21 Love, *McDonald's*, 54.

22 Ibid., 53.

23 Ibid.

24 James M. McLamore, *The Burger King: Jim McLamore and the Building of an Empire* (New York: McGraw-Hill, 1997).

25 Benjamin Wallace, "The Quest to Perfect the American Burger," *New York* magazine, June 1, 2015, http://www.grubstreet.com/2015/05/the-story-of-the-hamburger.html (Accessed February 28, 2017).

26 Ross, "Patterns."

27 Hogan, *Selling 'em by the Sack*, 175.

28 "Restaurant Burgers Had A Banner Year in 2014, Reports NPD," https://www.npd.com/wps/portal/npd/us/news/press-releases/2015/restaurant-burgers-had-a-banner-year-in-2014/ (Accessed March 4, 2017).

29 "Best and Worst Fast-Food restaurants in America. Chew Over the Results from Consumer Reports' Latest ReaderSurvey," *Consumer Reports*, July 2014, http://www.consumerreports.org/cro/magazine/2014/08/best-and-worst-fast-food-restaurants-in-america/index.htm (Accessed February 12, 2017).

30 USDA Standard of Identity for Hamburger, 299, https://www.gpo.gov/fdsys/pkg/CFR-2012-title9-vol2/pdf/CFR-2012-title9-vol2-part319.pdf (Accessed March 16, 2017).

31 Love, *McDonald's*, 130.

32 Hogan, *Selling 'em by the Sack*, p. 32.

Chapter 3

1 Velten, *Cow*, 27.

2 Ibid.

3 Rozin, *The Primal Cheeseburger*, 35–36.

4 http://www.leanandtenderbeef.com/About-Criollo-Cattle/Criollo-Cattle-History/ (Accessed March 2, 2017).

5 Velten, *Cow*, 28.

6 William Cronon, *Changes in the Land: Indians, Colonists, and the Ecology of New England* (New York: Hill and Wang, 1983), 139.

7 Cronon, *Changes in the Land*, 147.

8 George P. Marsh, *Man and Nature; or Physical Geography as Modified by Human Action* (New York: Charles Scribner, 1864), 364.

9 Virginia DeJohn Anderson, *Creatures of Empire: How Domestic Animals Transformed Early America* (Oxford and New York: Oxford University Press, 2004), 84.

10 George M. Beard, *Sexual Neurasthenia [Nervous Exhaustion]: Its Hygiene, Causes, Symptoms and Treatment with a Chapter on Diet for the Nervous* (New York: E. B. Treat and Co., 1898. Reprint, New York: Arno Press, 1972), 272.

11 Reviel Netz, *Barbed Wire: An Ecology of Modernity* (Middletown, CT: Wesleyan University Press, 2004), 48.

12 Netz, *Barbed Wire*, 49.

13 Ross, "Patterns," 198.

14 William Cronon, *Nature's Metropolis: Chicago and the Great West* (New York: Norton and Co., 1991), 212.

15 Ross, "Patterns," 200.

16 Paraphrasing Ross, "Patterns," 201.

17 Ross, "Patterns," 204.

18 George Catlin, quoted in Cronon, *Nature's Metropolis*, 215.

19 Cronon, *Nature's Metropolis*, 216.

20 Ibid., 217.

21 Ross, "Patterns," 199, quoting E. Dale in *The Range Cattle Industry: Ranching on the Great Plains from 1865–1925* (Norman; University of Oklahoma, 1960), 14.

22 Cronon, *Nature's Metropolis*, 220.

23 Netz, *Barbed Wire*, 1.

24 Ibid., xii.

25 Cronon, *Nature's Metropolis*, 259.

26 Ross, "Patterns," 204.

27 Ibid., 214.

28 Sinclair, *The Jungle*.

29 Eric Schlosser, *Fast Food Nation* (New York: Perennial, 2003), 171.

30 Schlosser, *Fast Food Nation*, 172.

31 Peter Lovenheim, *Portrait of a Burger as Young Calf* (New York: Three Rivers Press, 2002), 238–39.

32 Schlosser, *Fast Food Nation*, 204.

33 Ross, "Patterns," 247.

34 Lovenheim, "Portrait of a Burger," 190.

35 Michael Pollan, "Power Steer," *New York Times Magazine*, March 31, 2002, http://michaelpollan.com/articles-archive/power-steer/ (Accessed February 15, 2017).

36 Schlosser, *Fast Food Nation*, 153.

37 Ibid., 154.

38 "Blood, Sweat and Fear: Workers' Rights in U.S. Meat and Poultry Plants," A Human Rights Watch Report 2004,

http://www.hrw.org/reports/2005/usa0105/ (Accessed March 1, 2017).

39 Schlosser, *Fast Food Nation*, 172.

40 See Ross, "Patterns."

41 Samuel Zaffiri, *Hamburger Hill* (New York: Presidio Press, [1988], 1999), 171.

42 Zaffiri, *Hamburger Hill*, 273.

43 "The Battle for Hamburger Hill," *Time,* vol. 93, issue 22, (Accessed March 2, 2017).

44 Vasile Stănescu, "The Whopper Virgins: Hamburgers, Gender, and Xenophobia in Burger King's Hamburger Advertising," in *Meat Culture*, ed. Annie Potts (Leiden and Boston: Brill, 2016), 96.

45 Stănescu, "Whopper Virgins," 90–91.

Chapter 4

1 Ingram, *All This from a 5-Cent Hamburger!*, 11.

2 Philip Roth, *Portnoy's Complaint* (New York, 1973), 35.

3 Love, *McDonald's*, 129.

4 Schlosser, *Fast Food Nation*, 205.

5 Definitions from J. E. Lighter, *Random House Historical Dictionary of American Slang* (New York: Random House, 1994).

6 http://www.urbandictionary.com/define.php?term=on%twentiethe%20grind (Accessed March 2, 2017).

7 Jaik Puppyteeth, "The VICE Guide to Grindr," *Vice*, December 8, 2016, https://www.vice.com/en_us/article/how-to-be-good-at-grindr (Accessed March 15, 2017).

8 Hogan, *Selling 'em by the Sack*, 77–78.

9 Quoted in Dolores Hayden, *The Grand Domestic Revolution: A History of Feminist Designs for American Homes, Neighborhoods, and Cities* (Cambridge, MA: MIT Press, 1981), 207.

10 Quoted in *Redesigning the American Dream: The Future of Housing, Work, and Family Life* (New York: W. W. Norton, 1984), 82.

11 Hayden, *Redesigning the American Dream*, p. 68.

12 "Give Mother a Night Off" White Castle poster from the 1930s, White Castle System, Inc. Records, file AL03446.tif, http://www.ohiomemory.org/cdm/singleitem/collection/p15005coll29/id/204/rec/1 (Accessed May 16, 2017).

13 Love, *McDonald's*, 308.

14 Philip Langdon, *Orange Roofs, Golden Arches: The Architecture of American Chain Restaurants* (New York: Alfred A. Knopf, 1986), 156.

15 "The Thick Burger" was from Hardee's and Carl's Jr., "The Whopper" from Burger King, "The Big Mac" from McDonalds, the "Big Boy" from the chain known as Big Boy. "The Chubby Boy" and "Beefy Boy" were available in California during the time that Bob Wian developed the "Big Boy" for his restaurant; Ozersky, 48.

16 http://www.mrbartley.com/mrbartleys-menu.html (Accessed February 15, 2017).

17 Ronald L. McDonald, *The Complete Hamburger: The History of America's Favorite Sandwich* (Secaucus, NJ: Carol Publishing Group, 1997), xii.

18 Seth Stevenson, "Porn, Again: Another Lewd, Suggestive Ad for Meat," *Slate*, http://www.slate.com/articles/business/ad_report_card/2005/01/porn_again.html (Accessed February 16, 2017).

19 John Berger, *Ways of Seeing* (New York: Penguin Books, 1972), 47.

20 Claire Landsbaum, "Donald Trump's Pick for Labor Secretary Defended His Company's Sexist Ads," *New York Magazine: The Cut*, December 8, 2016, http://nymag.com/thecut/2016/12/trumps-labor-secretary-defended-his-companys-sexist-ads.html (Accessed May 19, 2017).

21 Laura Bates, "'Ugly women don't sell burgers'–the Trickle-Down Effect of Team Trump," *Guardian*, January 18, 2017, www.theguardian.com/us-news/2017/jan/18/trickle-down-effect-team-trumps-labour-secretary-nominee-andrew-puzder. See also Oliver Laughland and Lauren Gambino, "Restaurants Run by Labor Secretary Nominee Report 'Disturbing' Rates of Sexual Harassment," *Guardian*, www.theguardian.com/business/2017/jan/10/andrew-puzder-cke-sexual-harassment-labor-secretary?CMP=Share_iOSApp_Other#img-1 January 10, 2017 (Accessed January 28, 2017).

22 Candy Sagon, "He Eats, She Eats," *Washington Post*, June 7, 2006, http://www.washingtonpost.com/wpdyn/content/article/2006/06/06/AR2006060600304.html (Accessed March 3, 2017).

Chapter 5

1 John Darnton, "British Beef Sales Plunge as Germany and Italy Join Import Ban," *New York Times*, March 23, 1996, page 3.

2 Carol J. Adams, *The Sexual Politics of Meat: A Feminist-Vegetarian Critical Theory* (London and New York: Bloomsbury Revelations, 2015), 73.

3 Quoted in Robert B. Downs, afterword to *The Jungle*, 346.

4 David J. Wolfson, "McLibel," *Animal Law* 21, no. 5 (1999), available at http://www.mcspotlight.org/case/trial/verdict/wolfson2.html (Accessed March 15, 2017). Unless otherwise noted, all quotations in this section on McLibel are from Wolfson.

5 Space does not allow a complete summary of the case, the judge's ruling, the appeals, and the further appeals to the European Court of Human Rights that ruled that Steel and Morris had been denied a fair trial because they were not provided with legal representation.

6 Alicia Prygoski, "Detailed Discussion of Ag-gag Laws," *Michigan State University College of Law*, 2015, www.animallaw.info/article/detailed-discussion-ag-gag-laws (Accessed January 22, 2017).

7 Prygoski, "Detailed Discussion of Ag-gag Laws."

8 Specifically: National Association for Biomedical Research, Fur Commission USA, GlaxoSmithKline, Pfizer, Wyeth, United Egg Producers, National Cattlemen's Beef Association, and many more; "Animal Enterprise Terrorism 101," November 17, 2007, www.greenisthenewred.com/blog/aeta-101/313/ (Accessed January 23, 2017).

9 Will Potter, *Green is the New Red: An Insider's Account of a Social Movement Under Siege* (San Francisco: City Lights Books, 2011), 128.

10 Potter, 169.

11 Center for Constitutional Freedom, *The Animal Enterprise Terrorism Act (AETA)*, November 19, 2007, ccrjustice.

org/home/get-involved/tools-resources/fact-sheets-and-faqs/animal-enterprise-terrorism-act-aeta (Accessed January 23, 2017).

12 Howard F. Lyman, *Mad Cowboy: Plain Truth from the Cattle Rancher Who Won't Eat Meat* (New York: Scribner, 1998), 14–15.

13 Jeremy Rifkin, *Beyond Beef: The Rise and Fall of the Cattle Culture* (New York: Dutton Book, 1992), 200–12.

14 Eliza Barclay, "A Nation of Meat Eaters: See How It all Adds Up," *Morning Edition*, National Public Radio, June 27, 2012, http://www.npr.org/sections/thesalt/2012/06/27/155527365/visualizing-a-nation-of-meat-eaters (Accessed February 13, 2017).

15 Chelsea Harvey, "We are Killing the Environment One Hamburger at a Time," *Business Insider*, March 5, 2015, http://www.businessinsider.com/one-hamburger-environment-resources-2015-2 (Accessed February 13, 2017).

16 *Livestock's Long Shadow: Environmental Issues and Options,* The Livestock, Environment and Development Initiative, xxi, ftp://ftp.fao.org/docrep/fao/010/a0701e/a0701e.pdf (Accessed March 19, 2017).

17 Peter Singer, "No More Excuses," in Tim Flannery, *Now or Never: Why We Must Act Now to End Climate Change and Create a Sustainable Future* (New York: Atlantic Monthly Press, 2009), 131–42; Quoting in this instance Janet Raloff, "AAAS: Carbon-Friendly Dining . . . Meats," http://www.sciencenews.org/view/generic/id/40934/title/ AAAS_Climate-friendly_dining_%E2%80%A6_meats.

18 Joe Yonan, "The Shockingly Beeflike Veggie Burger that's not Aimed at Vegetarians," *Washington Post*, June 28, 2016, https://www.washingtonpost.com/lifestyle/food/the-shockingly-beeflike-veggie-burger-thats-not-aimed-at-vegetarians/2016/06/27/e483a9fa-3c6a-11e6-80bc-d06711fd2125_story.html?utm_term=.7b6618a83ac8 (Accessed February 13, 2017).

19 Lisa Kemmerer, *Eating Earth: Environmental Ethics and Dietary Choice* (London and New York: Oxford University Press, 2015), 14.

20 Julia Rosen, "Why Your Hamburger Might Be Leading to Nitrogen Pollution," *The Salt: What's On Your Plate*, National Public Radio, February 25, 2016, http://www.npr.org/sections/thesalt/2016/02/25/467962593/why-your-hamburger-might-be-leading-to-nitrogen-pollution (Accessed March 10, 2017).

21 Nick Fiddes, *Meat: A Natural Symbol* (London and New York: Routledge, 1991), 65.

22 "Food that we feed to food" is a statement made by Christopher Schlottmann.

23 Kemmerer, *Eating Earth*, 10.

24 KeShun Liu, *Soybeans: Chemistry, Technology, and Utilization* (New York: Chapman and Hall, 1997), 427.

25 Schlosser, *Fast Food Nation*, 197.

26 Debora Mackenzie, "Antibiotic Resistance Hits Crisis Point," *New Scientist* 14 (December 2016), https://www.newscientist.com/article/mg23231044-000-antibiotic-resistance-will-hit-a-terrible-tipping-point-in-2017/ (Accessed January 17, 2017).

Chapter 6

1 K. Annabelle Smith, "The History of the Veggie Burger," *Smithsonian.com*, http://www.smithsonianmag.com/arts-culture/history-veggie-burger-180950163/ (Accessed November 15, 2016).

2 Mildred Lager, *The Useful Soybean: A Plus Factor in Modern Living* (New York: McGraw-Hill Book Co., 1945), 177.

3 "Weights and Wacky Dieting," *Arizona Daily Star*, March 12, 1961, page 44.

4 Kay Canter and Daphne Swann, *Entertaining with Cranks* (J. M. Dent and Sons, Ltd., 1985), 107.

5 Davidson, *The Oxford Companion to Food,* 238.

6 Ibid., 229.

7 M. R. L. Sharpe, *The Golden Rule Cookbook: Six Hundred Recipes for Meatless Dishes* (Cambridge: The University Press, 1907), 180.

8 Toby C. Wilkinson, Susan Sheratt, and John Bennet, eds., *Interweaving Worlds: Systemic Interactions in Eurasia, 7th to 1st Millenia BC* (Oxford and Oakville: Oxbow Books, 2011), 52.

9 K. T. Achaya, *Indian Food: A Historical Companion* (Delhi: Oxford University Press, 1994), 290.

10 William Shurtleff and Akiko Aoyagi, *The Book of Tofu: Food for Mankind* (Kanagawa-Ken, Japan: Autumn Press, 1975), v, 269.

11 Ronald L. Numbers, *Prophetess of Health: A Study of Ellen G. White* (New York: Harper & Row, 1976), 81.

12 This history is indebted to the exhaustive history offered by *History of Meat Alternatives (HMA)*, specifically, page 6.

13 HMA #61; Ella Ervilla Eaton Kellogg, *Healthful Cookery: A collection of choice recipes for preparing foods, with special reference to health* (Battle Creek, MI: Modern Medicine Publishing Co., 1940), https://babel.hathitrust.org/cgi/imgsrv/download/pdf?id=nyp.33433082242813;orient=0;size=100;seq=103;num=99;attachment=0 (Accessed from NY Public Library).

14 HMA #251.

15 Hogan, *Selling 'em by the Sack,* 104.

16 Ibid., 107.

17 HMA #265; "Soybeans Protein Rich: Vegetable May Substitute in Food Value for Hamburger," *New York Times*, May 23, 1943, section 8, page 6.2.

18 HMA #286; Jane Holt, "News of Food: Soy Grits are Utilized in New Mixture," *New York Times*, January 10, 1944, page 14.2, (Accessed March 4, 2017).

19 HMA #291; Clementine Paddleford, "Food for Conversation," *Los Angeles Times*, March 12, 1944, page F14.

20 Richard L. Hittleman, *Be Young with Yoga* (New York: Prentice-Hall, 1962), 210.

21 HMA #6211.

22 "Low-cost Soybeans: 'Meat that Grows on Vines,'" *Christian Science Monitor*, January 16, 1975, page 11; Excerpted in William Shurtleff and Akiko Aoyagi, *History of Soybean Crushing (980-2016)*, http://www.soyinfocenter.com/pdf/196/Crus.pdf (Accessed March 7, 2017)—hereafter "Crushing," #676; Norman H. Fischer, "Beanburgers–More Americans turn to Soybean Products as Meat Substitutes: Restaurants, Stores Find Consumers like the Taste and Especially the Price," *Wall Street Journal*, April 3, 1973, page 1, col. 1; "Crushing," p. 2509.

23 William Shurtleff and Akiko Aoyagi, *Book of Tofu*, 61.

24 *Indianapolis Star*, November 20, 1977.

25 HMA #2761; Marian Burros, "When Tofu Meets Bun: Eating Well," *New York Times*, January 4, 1995, pages C1, C6.

26 HMA #983; Ron Rosenbaum, "The Alternative Big Mac," *Esquire*, April 1983, 126.

27 "Crushing," 5.

28 Brian Palmer, "Is Your Veggie Burger Killing You?" *Slate*, April 2010, http://www.slate.com/articles/news_and_politics/ explainer/2010/04/is_your_veggie_burger_killing_you.html (Accessed February 17, 2017).

29 HMA #689; Daniel S. Greenberg, "Slaughterhouse Zero: How Soybean Sellers Plan to Take the Animal Out of Meat," *Harper's*, November 1973, 38–43.

30 HMA #784; Liz Roman Gallese, "Soy is Rebounding as a Substitute for Animal Protein," *Wall Street Journal*, June 4, 1975, page 24.

31 Barry G. Swanson, "Hexane Extraction in Soy Food Processing," http://www.soyfoods.org/wp-content/uploads/ Regulatory%20Expert%20Document-Barry%20Swanson%20 revised.pdf (Accessed February 17, 2017).

32 Atish Patel, "The Jackfruit Patty? Vegetarian Burger Options for President Obama," *Wall Street Journal*, January 25, 2015,http://blogs.wsj.com/indiarealtime/2015/01/25/the- jackfruit-patty-vegetarian-burger-options-for-president- obama/ (Accessed March 3, 2017).

33 Georgie Bronte, "Green Jackfruit: Is 'pulled pork for vegetarians' the next big food craze?" *Guardian*, April 12, 2015, https://www.theguardian.com/lifeandstyle/ shortcuts/2015/apr/12/green-jackfruit-vegetable-pulled-pork (Accessed March 3, 2017).

Chapter 7

1 Margaret Rouse, "Moonshot," http://whatis.techtarget.com/ definition/moonshot (Accessed May 17, 2017).

2 The other five were 3D printing for buildings, "'augmenting reality,' or adding visual and audio cues in environments like cars, in the workplace or in education," mobile phones for "monitoring personal health and for collecting health data," self-driving cars, and fixing education using technology. Katie Fehrenbacher, "The 6 Most Important Tech Trends, According to Eric Schmidt," *Fortune*, May 2, 2016, http://fortune.com/2016/05/02/eric-schmidts-6-tech-trends/ (Accessed May 16, 2017).

3 Janay Laing, "Get Ready for a Meat Revolution," June 1, 2016, https://medium.com/food-is-the-new-internet/get-ready-for-a-meat-revolution-df21cd27c7fc (Accessed May 16, 2017).

4 Rowan Jacobsen, "This Top-Secret Food will Change the Way You Eat," December 26, 2014, https://www.outsideonline.com/1928211/top-secret-food-will-change-way-you-eat (Accessed May 17, 2017).

5 Unless otherwise noted, quotations in this chapter are from: Pat Brown, Media Day at Impossible Foods, Redwood City, CA., February 7, 2017; Ethan Brown, visit to Beyond Meat, El Segundo, Ca., March 9, 2017; Uma Valeti, "Waking Up with Sam Brown," Episode #28, "Meat Without Misery: A Conversation with Uma Valeti," https://soundcloud.com/samharrisorg/meat-without-murder (Accessed March 16, 2017); Bruce Friedrich, Conversation, Los Angeles, California, March 9, 2017.

6 Stephanie Strom, "Tyson Foods, a Meat Leader, Invests in Protein Alternatives," October 10, 2016, https://futurism.com/lab-grown-meat-tyson-is-making-a-massive-investment-in-a-meatless-future/ (Accessed March 17, 2017).

7 Melia Robinson, "Google Wanted to Buy this Startup that Makes Fake Meat—Here's why the CEO Will Never Sell," March

27, 2017, http://www.businessinsider.com/impossible-foods-google-acquisition-rumors-2017-3 (Accessed May 16, 2017).

8 Jacobsen, "This Top-Secret Food."

9 Jonathan Kauffman, "Impossible Burger Debut: A Non-Meat Patty for Carnivores," *San Francisco Chronicle*, October12, 2016, http://www.sfchronicle.com/food/article/Impossible-Burger-debut-A-non-meat-patty-for-9967111.php (Accessed March 6, 2017).

10 Nathan Myhrvold, "The Maillard Reaction," *Modernist Cuisine*, March 20, 2013, http://modernistcuisine.com/2013/03/the-maillard-reaction/ (Accessed March 9, 2017).

11 Bruce Friedrich, "'Clean Meat': The 'Clean Energy' of Food," *Good Food Institute*, September 6, 2016, http://www.gfi.org/clean-meat-the-clean-energy-of-food (Accessed March 16, 2017).

12 Isha Datar with help from Daan Luining, "Mark Post's Cultured Beef," November 3, 2015, http://www.new-harvest.org/mark_post_cultured_beef (Accessed March 16, 2017).

13 Datar and Luining, "Mark Post's Cultured Beef."

14 Michael Specter, "Test-tube Burgers: How Long will it be Before you can Eat Meat that was made in a Lab?" *New Yorker*, May 23, 2011, http://www.newyorker.com/magazine/2011/05/23/test-tube-burgers (Accessed March 16, 2017).

15 Specter, "Test-tube Burgers."

16 Jacob Bunge, "Sizzling Steaks May Soon Be Lab-Grown: Startups Raising Funds to Produce Meat from Cells Cultivated in Bioreactors," *Wall Street Journal*, February 1, 2016, https://www.wsj.com/articles/sizzling-steaks-may-soon-be-lab-grown-1454302862 (Accessed March 17, 2017).

17 Clean meat faces some specific challenges in terms of growth. Emily Byrd identified them as creating immortal cell lines that can be used indefinitely, developing animal-free media (nutrients) instead of animal-based serum as a food source for cells' replication; scaffolding for the cells to grow to match the texture, taste, and look of conventionally produced meat, and larger bioreactors in which the growth occurs. Emily Byrd, "Clean Meat's Path to Your Dinner Plate," *Good Food Institute blog*, December 7, 2016, http://www.gfi.org/clean-meats-path-to-commercialization (Accessed May 18, 2017).

18 Annie Sciacca, "Oakland: 'Impossible' Meatless Burgers Ramp up Production at New Facility," *East Bay Times*, March 23, 2017, http://www.eastbaytimes.com/2017/03/23/oakland-impossible-meatless-burgers-ramp-up-production-at-new-facility/ (Accessed May 16, 2017).

19 Craig Giammona, "Bill Gates-Backed Vegan Burgers Hit Mainstream with Safeway Deal," Bloomberg, May 25, 2017, https://www.bloomberg.com/news/articles/2017-05-25/bill-gates-backed-vegan-burgers-hit-mainstream-with-safeway-deal (Accessed May 25, 2017).

20 http://www.newcropcapital.com/ (Accessed May 18, 2017).

21 For a general overview, see Adams, *The Sexual Politics of Meat*.

22 This is something he and I discussed when I met him in March. The quotation is from "Silicon Valley Gets a Taste for Food," *Economist*, March 7, 2015, https://store.eiu.com/article.aspx?productid=220000222&articleid=822942066 (Accessed May 18, 2017).

23 Nick Solares, "Bleeding Veggie Burger Makes an Appearance in a New Lunch Dish at Momofuku Ssam Bar," *Eater*, January 18, 2017, http://ny.eater.com/2017/1/18/14298660/

impossible-burger-momomfuku-ssam-bar-momofuku-nishi (Accessed February 14, 2017).

24 Jacobsen, "This Top-Secret Food."

Afterword: *Slippage*

1 Jeff Gordinier, "Sharing an Ayurvedic Lunch with a Yogi," *New York Times*, February 9, 2011, https://dinersjournal. blogs.nytimes.com/2011/02/09/sharing-an-ayurvedic-lunch-with-a-yogi/?rref=collection%2Fbyline%2Fjeff-gordinierand action=clickandcontentCollection=undefinedandregion=str eamandmodule=stream_unitandversion=latestandcontentPl acement=351andpgtype=collection (Accessed December 17, 2016).

2 Jeff Gordinier, "For Actresses, Is a Big Appetite Part of the Show?" *New York Times*, February 15, 2011.

3 Jeff Gordinier, "Masters of Disguise Among Meatless Burgers," *New York Times*, March 23, 2011, http://www.nytimes. com/2011/03/23/dining/23meatless.html (Accessed March 3, 2017).

4 Jeff Gordinier, "Come Back, Veggie Burger. All Is Forgiven," *New York Times*, March 22, 2011, https://dinersjournal.blogs. nytimes.com/2011/03/22/come-back-veggie-burger-all-is-forgiven/ (Accessed March 3, 2017).

5 Andy Husbands, Chris Hart, and Andrea Pyenson, *Wicked Good Burgers: Fearless Recipes and Uncompromising Techniques for the Ultimate Patty* (Beverly, MA: Fair Winds Press, 2013), 115.

6 Ronald L. McDonald, *The Complete Hamburger: The History of America's Favorite Sandwich* (Secaucus, NY: Carol Publishing Group, 1997), xv.

7 Observation made by Christopher Schlottmann.

8 Alan Thein Durning and Holly B. Brough, "Reforming the Livestock Economy," in *State of the World: A Worldwatch Institute Report on Progress Toward a Sustainable Society*, ed. Lester R. Brown et al. (New York: Norton and Co, 1992), 80.

9 HMA #689; Daniel S. Greenberg, "Slaughterhouse Zero: How Soybean Sellers Plan to Take the Animal Out of Meat," *Harper's* 247, November 1973, 38–43.

10 Alton Brown, "The End of Meat as We Know It," *Wired*, September 17, 2013, http://www.wired.com/2013/09/fakemeat/ (Accessed March 3, 2017).

11 John Lockett, "The Best Burger of the Year Has No Meat in It," *GQ*, October 29, 2015, http://www.gq.com/story/best-burger-of-the-year-superiority-burger (Accessed March 3, 2017).

12 Elizabeth G. Dunn, "Where's the Beet? Veggie Burgers Even Carnivores Will Crave," *Wall Street Journal*, October 20, 2015, https://www.wsj.com/articles/wheres-the-beet-veggie-burgers-even-carnivores-will-crave-1445371914 (Accessed March 3, 2017).

INDEX